HAND TOOLS

Series editor: Frédérique Crestin-Billet
Design: Lélie Carnot
Translated from the French by Jonathan Sly
Copyediting: Linda Gardiner
Typesetting: Thierry Renard
Proofreading: Kate Lancaster and Mark Hunt
Color separation by Chesteroc Graphics
Printed in Singapore

Distributed in North America by Rizzoli International Publications, Inc.

Originally published as La Folie des Outils © Flammarion 2002
English-language edition © Flammarion 2004

Flammarion
87, quai Panhard et Levassor
75647 Paris Cedex 13

www.editions.flammarion.com

06 07 3 2
ISBN: 978-2-0803-0438-4

Dépôt legal: 03/2004

Collectible
HAND TOOLS

Dominique Pascal

Flammarion

This book is dedicated to my grandfather, a mason, who walked with his brother from their village of Peyrat-le-Château in search of work in the nearest city, Lyons, 220 miles away to the east. He found a job in Saint-Symphorien-d'Ozon. And to my godfather, who set off from his home village of Saint-Nicolas-d'Aliermont to look for work in Paris. He became a fitter at an Anzani factory, the pioneering engine and engine-part manufacturer.

And to my father-in-law, who had a car repair shop in the rue du Chevaleret in Paris. And to Raoul Moulin, a miller from Septeuil, to the east of Paris, who offered me the hand tools belonging to his father, a saddler from nearby Houdan. He had cleaned, oiled, and tidied them away before leaving to fight in the Great War. He never returned. And to Maurice Lemarié, a joiner in Montchauvet. All these men wielded their tools with talent, conscientiousness, and love, and took immense pride in their lives as working craftsmen.

CONTENTS

Introduction

Hand tools are such uncomplicated things, made of simple materials—wood, iron, steel, horn, or leather—yet so sophisticated in their conception. In today's world where electronics permeate everything, converting ever more worshippers to their new religion, it is hard to envisage what role hand tools have left to play. In factories in industrialized countries, nails are no longer driven by hammer, but by machines, bristling with sharp steel tips that thrust through the hardest materials like a knife through butter. A rare sight it is to watch a pair of expert hands shave long curls from a strip of rosewood using a trying plane. Nowadays, computer-programmed blades, calibrated to within a thousandth of an inch, do the work for us.

T he world has seen the evolution of industrial progress, leading to new knowledge and skills, from the moment the first stone tool was hewn to the Silicon Valley revolution. This book thumbs its nose at high-tech, computerized, robot technology and celebrates the tools of yesterday and the people who still wield them, whenever modern life leaves them the time. The tool collector, in this situation, is like a fisherman with no time to find the richest fishing spots, who compensates for his frustration by gathering the finest fly-fishing rods, the most sophisticated American-made lures and Scottish-fashioned reels together in a closet. A beautiful antique implement that may look like no more than a miscellaneous chunk of wood or steel may turn up in a flea market and find its way home for no particular reason. Or maybe the intention is only too deliberate. For an old tool is like a good bottle of wine: it has to be right there, within arm's reach, for the exact moment it is needed.

It takes only a Goldenberg drawknife, immediately recognizable, and several gouges from Sheffield, England, and the carving begins to take shape. Antique tools, while collected for their beauty, should not just sit idle.

In the case of wine or champagne, that moment may be provided by a friend who drops in, a happy occasion or a bad day. With a tool, however, that joyous moment may arrive when you want to clean up a complicated curved edge at the bottom of a slightly damaged antique wardrobe you've just acquired. For the first time, you are going to be able to call upon that router you purchased so long ago, which has lain forgotten ever since at the back of a drawer. You may be left wondering if the tool itself did not have some influence in your decision, urging you on to buy chipped furniture, whispering in your ear that it wants to see daylight and rattle its blade.

This page: the knife grinder pumping his whetstone with his foot is sharpening the edge of a knife. Facing page: Plane irons must also undergo whetstone treatment. Another important part of collecting tools is mastering the difficult art of sharpening.

P robably all French tool collectors,
from those who own thousands to
those who take great pleasure in
using but a handful of antique tools
without cluttering their shelves, have,
at some point in their youth, set their
hands on specialist catalogs—such as that
of "Manufacture d'armes et cycles de Saint-
Étienne," the Saint-Étienne gun and bicycle
factory. Who knows why the "Les fils de
Peugeot Frères" catalog from 1899,
for example, was still hanging around
in our family library some sixty years after
it was printed, lurking among the period's
bestsellers, biographies of explorers and tales
of bucolic life? I thank my parents for keeping
our cherry bookshelves (and my head) free
from complicated tomes of philosophy
and obscure foreign writers, or I might
never have found it.

JARDINIER
CHOCOLAT POULAIN

The history of tool-making started at home, before village blacksmiths took charge of their manufacture. With the arrival of the industrial age, supply was assured by manufacturers and wholesalers who produced billboards and catalogs featuring their wares categorized by trade.

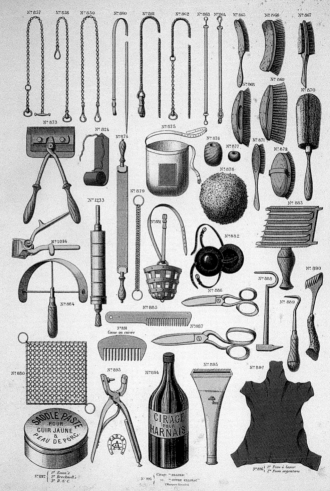

This Peugeot catalog became my bedside reading, and rather than pore over my multiplication tables, I learned the prices of workbenches off by heart, as well as their captions, such as "Benches number 2 and 3 are larger and wider than number 1 and answer to all the amateur joiner's needs. Like number 1, they contain a complete selection of choice hand tools."

The Saint-Étienne guns and cycles factory has, for over a century, manufactured a variety of tools including a cornucopia of planes for all sorts of applications.

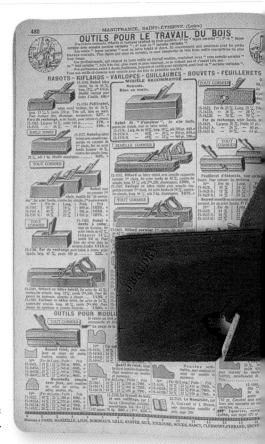

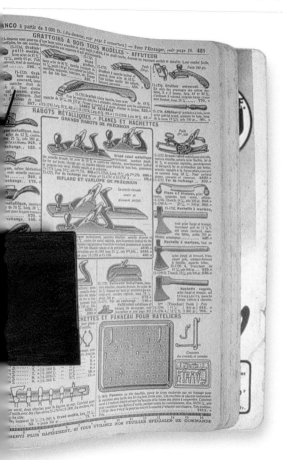

When I was ten,
I could spend hours and
hours soaking up pages
178 and 179, dreaming
of new and beautiful
things—of shiny
handles, with their
little labels attached;
of gleaming blades free
of snags; of the endless
possibilities for carving
extraordinary pieces that
would be the pride and
joy of Mom and Dad and
the rest of the family
besides. Another
enchanting page of
the catalog was number
184. Here, under
the column heading
"Peugeot tool boxes

and cases," is Model 1. "Model 1" deserves its capital M,
such was the appeal of this extraordinary case that triggered
so many dreams and desires in my child's mind. It was,
the caption states, "Especially produced to enable explorers,
settlers and long-distance travelers to transport, in the minimum
of space necessary, a complete collection of daily utility tools."
A case for special tools for discovering distant continents,
made of varnished walnut, and all for only 250 francs. I
imagined the great colonists and explorers—Pierre
Savorgnan de Brazza (1852–1905) and Robert
Baden-Powell (1857–1941)—deep in the heart
of Africa, sallying forth foolhardily into
unknown lands with the case attached
to a backpack,
clattering
along to
the trudge
of the
bearer's
feet.

The smell of roasting horn as the blacksmith, sleeves rolled up, quickly shoes an impatient horse, is a memorable one. This cover of the magazine *Rustica*, a weekly publication specializing in country life, dated March 1950, depicts what was still an everyday scene at the time, even though mechanization was very much on the move. Facing page: a plane from the same period as the magazine.

What was wonderful about this catalog was the huge range of products and varieties. There was not just one file but a whole array—flat files giving a rough cut, bastard cut, second cut, or smooth cut, three inches to a foot and a half long, imperial measures still being the standard. Files could be pointed, half-round or round, square-tipped, warding, crossing or equaling. The possibilities were endless. Reading a catalog is also about understanding that each trade has its own tools and that there are as many pitchforks as there are trowels. Hammers proliferate yet more; every craft has its own varieties—the farrier, stone-cutter, even the glazier.

Catalogs were essential to the supply of tools to the more remote parts of rural France. They replaced peddlers who, from the Middle Ages onwards, had supplied consumer goods. Here is a page from the Aux Mines de Suède catalog, the famous, now defunct, European tool manufacturers.

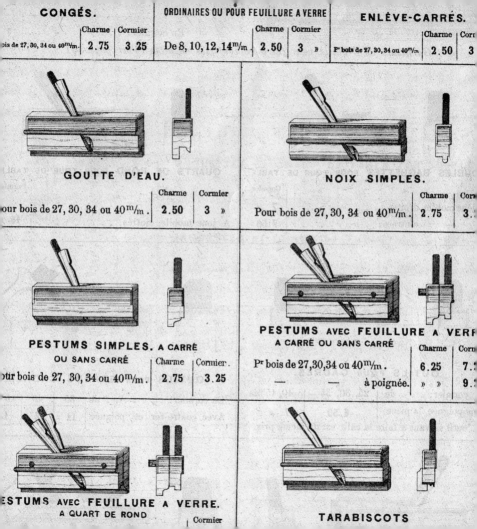

CONGÉS.			ORDINAIRES OU POUR FEUILLURE A VERRE			ENLÈVE-CARRÉS.		
	Charme	Cormier		Charme	Cormier		Charme	Corm
bois de 27, 30, 34 ou 40 m/m.	2.75	3.25	De 8, 10, 12, 14 m/m .	2.50	3 »	Pr bois de 27, 30, 34 ou 40 m/m	2.50	3

GOUTTE D'EAU.

	Charme	Cormier
our bois de 27, 30, 34 ou 40 m/m.	2.50	3 »

NOIX SIMPLES.

	Charme	Corm
Pour bois de 27, 30, 34 ou 40 m/m.	2.75	3.

PESTUMS SIMPLES. A CARRÉ
OU SANS CARRÉ

	Charme	Cormier.
otir bois de 27, 30, 34 ou 40 m/m.	2.75	3.25

PESTUMS AVEC FEUILLURE A VERR
A CARRÉ OU SANS CARRÉ

	Charme	Corm
Pr bois de 27, 30, 34 ou 40 m/m .	6.25	7.
— — à poignée.	» »	9.

ESTUMS AVEC FEUILLURE A VERRE.
A QUART DE ROND
Cormier

TARABISCOTS

Models abound, each with its own specific use or very general application: a round peen on one side, flat on the other, is all-important for clinching nails; the packer's hammer is split in two for pulling; there is the lath-hammer with its peens of different lengths; or the elegant tinsmith's hammer with the long beak of a curlew. Another important factor relating to shape is that of geographical origin. Take trowels, for example, such as the Philadelphia trowel with its wide heel, or the narrower London trowel. There are thousands of other tools that change depending on the country, region or city. Billhooks come in many

Bernard Solon is one of the last edge-tool craftsmen in France. He signs his tools Alexis and he is based in the heart of Orléans, to the southwest of Paris. This page; a pair of secateurs from Thiers, a hub of edge-tool manufacture in France.

varieties in France alone—even within relatively close areas such as Amiens, Rouen, Compiègne, or the Pas-de-Calais. Since the Iron Age, tools have slowly evolved in a Darwinian fashion, in specific isolated locations producing general forms. This is why Italian edge-tool makers had a different way of producing axes from those of Lyons or Paris, or why coopers' hammers to the north of Paris were not the same as those used in Mediterranean countries; coopers north and south had very different ways of working iron, as we shall see later. Different kinds of adze were developed in Naples, Astoria, Portugal, or Madrid.

Cultivating fields and gardens has given rise to a number of specific tools—rakes, forks, scythes, and sickles. Above is a pruning hook, a tool that folds up to fit in the gardener's pocket.

INTRODUCTION

For centuries, an apprentice craftsman would have to sweep out the workshop and do the shopping, deliveries, and household chores. In between, when not being bullied and insulted, his first job was to make his own tools. Such was workshop life for the lucky novice who actually managed to find a master craftsman to teach him how to become a master himself. He had to undergo a kind of initiation ritual similar to that of young Inuit seal hunters out on their first hunt, or that of African adolescents who are sent into the rainforests to fend for themselves. These tools, fashioned under the master's gaze, often stayed with the craftsman all his life, and were perfected as his skills increased. If he was lucky enough he would graduate from apprentice to journeyman, and adopt a trade nickname like "Rouennais La Bouche en Fleur" or "Périgord La Chance La Compagnie." Beyond the tools themselves, collectors show a love for the people who used them. The tool means nothing

This picture was taken in 1956. The apprentice is Daniel Lesoimier, from the La Roquelle craft school in the north of France. Today, he is the curator of the Musée d'Outil ancien, a museum of tools in Bièvres, France (address page 375). With the carpenter's emblematic mortising axe in hand and pride in his eye, the young man is about to embark on an exemplary career in this most noble of professions.

A hoe, with prongs, rather than a blade. The hoe family comes in a wide variety of shapes and sizes depending on their function —weeding, soil cultivation, digging or making furrows.

when taken out of context, out of the workshop and away from the skills, sweat, and labor of the craftsman. This is probably why, at specialized antique fairs, collectors and amateurs alike huddle around stalls asking simple or complex questions that all amount to the same thing: What was this for? Vendors and customers start talking, everyone joins in, people exchange reminiscences, minds whirr, and practical knowledge comes into play as together they investigate the characteristics of the objects in question, which may seem dull and meaningless to the uninitiated. It is worth noting that, from the nineteenth century onwards, while some tools began to be featured in lavish catalogs, making them more widely available, others were still created one at a time, at the back of the workshop, for specific uses with a short application life. It is these tools that pose the greatest problems of identification and generate the longest discussions and questioning. Here, the slightest signs or marks of wear and tear become invaluable clues.

A piece of advice: choose tools that are elegantly signed or stamped, like this large scythe.

Tools were the brainchild of early humans, ages and ages ago. Books featuring tools and their evolution or description generally start with a long disquisition on the fascinating history of the human race and its desire to extend the abilities of the hand. To give a simple notion of the slow evolution of human intelligence without going into vast detail, I provide a short summary taken from Alain Decaux's history of France for children, published by the Librairie académique Perrin in 1988 (still my favorite history book), supplemented by information from the *Larousse du XXe siècle*, 1920 edition. Human ancestors appeared in Africa five million

The adze dates back to the dawn of time. Its design has changed little over the ages. This bronze adze is from the Gallo-Roman period.

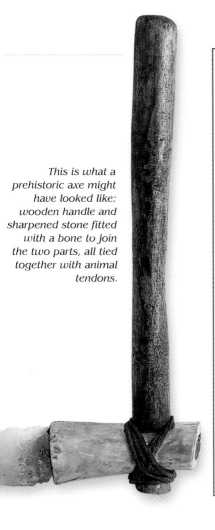

This is what a prehistoric axe might have looked like: wooden handle and sharpened stone fitted with a bone to join the two parts, all tied together with animal tendons.

Brief chronology

– *3.5 million years B.C.E.:* Good news: Australopithecus *primates learn to stand and sharpen flint and pebbles.*

– *1.5 million years B.C.E.:* Homo erectus *appears and refines stone-cutting techniques.*

– *1 million years B.C.E.:* Homo sapiens— *who knows how—master fire.*

– *40,000 years B.C.E.:* Homo sapiens *gain self-consciousness. This is the Paleolithic age, the age when stone was hewn with method and awareness. People start to sculpt and paint.*

– *c. 8,000 years B.C.E.: The Neolithic age—the era of polished stone— begins in Mesopotamia, 1500 years ahead of the West.*

– *5,500 B.C.E.: The Copper Age in the Middle East, preceding the Bronze Age.*

– *3,500 B.C.E.: Sumerians invent the wheel and, 500 years later, the swing-plough, a form of primitive plough.*

– *1,100 B.C.E.: Iron-working techniques spread from Asia Minor to Mesopotamia.*

years ago. They had small foreheads and protruding jaws; they were on average four feet (1.2 m) tall and had long hair, no doubt because they lacked the means to cut it. However, they would shortly learn to stand upright, a position that would enable them to surpass themselves and achieve greater things. Their first tools would no doubt have been sticks, for fighting, and pebbles, initially for breaking open shells and nuts, then for smashing other pebbles to produce sharp edges and points—tools were in the making.

Toiling in the fields in the Middle Ages. Scythes, forks, baskets, and whetstones and their sheaths, nothing really changed for centuries apart from a marked deterioration in the elegance of the harvesters.

Tools also send us messages. For millions of years, prehistoric people's housing and clothing were made of plant and animal matter. The only traces of their ways of life that remain are their hand tools, which come down to us like messages in bottles thrown into the sea. Their instruments were not just practical but solid, made of flint, bronze, and iron, and they have survived in large numbers to tell us much about their owners. Tell me how you work and what tools you use and I will tell you who you are. The fundamental tasks of cutting, sharpening, hitting, crushing, splitting, piercing, digging, adjusting, supporting, and measuring have all required special tools, whose direct descendants are to be found in the pages of this book, reflecting the genius of their makers.

Facing page: a goldsmith's workshop from the seventeenth century. Their guild, apart from making jewelry and other precious objects, also produced the first eyeglasses. On the left of the engraving you can see the jewelers' plates featured on page 197, for shaping and finishing precious metals. This page, a glass-cutting diamond with a brass handle from the nineteenth century.

I

FARMING
hand tools

U nder "Farming Hand Tools" we also include
tools used in gardening, winegrowing, and
animal breeding. The life of the countryside
has generated a vast range of equipment—especially
the tools needed to pick fruits, flowers, and
vegetables, to harvest crops in summer and grapes
in autumn. Animal breeding has given rise to so
many specialized tools that it is impossible to show
or even list them all, but some are included here.
Trees, impressive while they stand and still majestic
when they lie on the forest floor, require tools
to gauge, prune and fell them.

While one hand wields the sickle, the other wears this finger protection cup. It was invented by farmers and often made of sycamore.

It is hard to say exactly where this magnificent ash wood hayfork might come from. Note the tips of the prongs, capped with cow horn. The photo on page 38 features other reaping tools— three small anvils and a hammer for beating scythes.

This comb was used to gather clover flowers. The tray is not slatted because the seeds too were to be collected. Like the blueberry comb, facing page, the teeth of this comb are made of aluminum. Both date from the twentieth century.

Blueberry comb. This tool was common in areas such as the Alps where blueberries were abundant. The tool was used to literally comb the bushes and collect the berries in the tray fitted with metal rods. The blueberries were freed of any leaves or pieces of twig and then emptied into a milk churn fitted with straps for carrying back to the valley.

*Three
examples of
fruit-gathering
implements. The red model is
factory-made, while the green one,
far right, is handcrafted. These tools
were attached to a long handle and used
to reach the juiciest pears, figs, or cherries
on the highest branches of the tree.*

The stalk of the fruit would get caught in one of the grooves and, when the tool was raised, would snap from the tree. The fruit would then fall into the receptacle. These tools are fun to use and come in all sorts of shapes and materials—wicker, wood, zinc, wire mesh, and canvas.

This winegrowers' billhook was made by Imbert Cadet in Arles, in the south of France, and had two functions. The curved blade cut the vine while the axe blade cut or split the supporting poles.

Forged-steel winegrowers' secateurs. The handles are longer to help increase the force needed for cutting vine stock. They are also widely spaced so as not to pinch the hands if the blades suddenly slam closed.

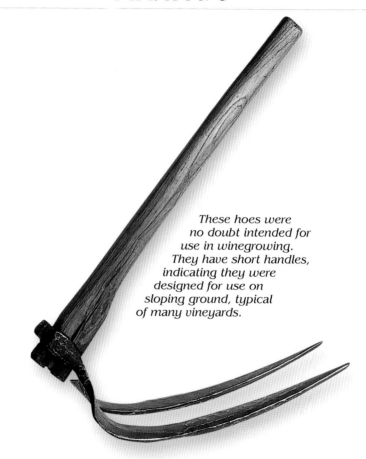

These hoes were no doubt intended for use in winegrowing. They have short handles, indicating they were designed for use on sloping ground, typical of many vineyards.

While the two-toothed hoe on the facing page is suitable for stony ground, this flat hoe is well adapted for turning soil with a higher clay content.

This heavy-duty corkscrew was used to pull the bungs from barrels. It is a cooper's bung borer and functions like a regular corkscrew—the gimlet screws into the wood while the two side-supports rest on the staves.

This is not an axe but a Burgundy marc cutter, used for breaking up the marc, or grape residue, packed at the bottom of winepresses. A wooden handle slips through the narrow ring, to enable the blade to rock back and forth over the residue.

This hoe was used on vineyards in an area of eastern France, to hoe the vine stock and possibly to aerate the vineyard soil in winter.

This hook is a tool still used today by woodcutters and in sawmills for shifting logs and tree-trunks. It sinks into the wood while the handle functions as a lever to roll the log over.

This decorative item has a brass frame, steel blade, and fine walnut handle. It is a grafting knife for winegrowing and features the manufacturer's name, Despujols. Such an implement was used to cut the grafts for vine cultivation. Before the appearance of phylloxera at the end of the nineteenth century, vines were cultivated by rooting stalks then severing them from the mother plant. When plants were imported from America to halt the disease, new grafting techniques were favored using tools of this kind.

This grafting knife has a dual purpose. Using the end of the tool gives a straight cut, the middle an oblique cut.

*These gouges or knives were used to harvest
delicately-flavored asparagus. Two kinds
of asparagus knife were in use—the upper
example, with its saw-tooth blade,
and the lower two, with their
gouge-like tips.*

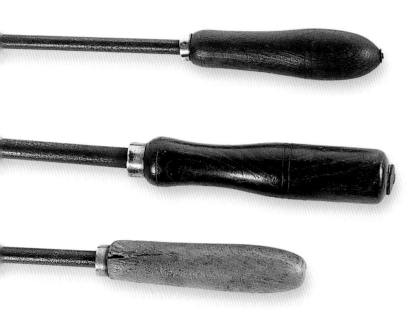

*Pruning saws of the non-folding variety
often have a small hook at the end of
the blade. This enables gardeners to hook
the tool to a branch when perched on a ladder
or high in the boughs so as to leave both
hands free for some particular task.
The handle of this one is made
of stag's horn.*

There are a whole host of folding garden
saws, in many shapes and sizes.
In the 1899 Peugeot Frères catalog,
they are identified as "knife-saws for
winegrowing" and were available
in eleven dimensions from six to
sixteen inches (16 to 40 cm).
Note that the teeth are
angled backwards,
to cut on the pull
rather than the
push stroke.

These two are both gardeners' folding saws. They have different teeth-sets designed for different uses, in orchards or vineyards. Some of these folding saws open automatically, like flick-knives.

This grafting knife was widespread in France and features in all the catalogs from the end of the nineteenth century onwards. It is equipped with the three implements necessary for grafting—a short steel saber-shaped blade, a longer pruning hook, and a spatula, made of bone or ivory. The blades were used to make the incision, and the spatula held the slit in the bark open to introduce the graft.

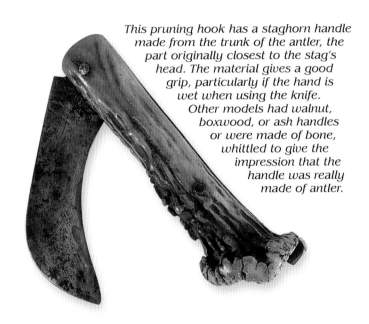

This pruning hook has a staghorn handle made from the trunk of the antler, the part originally closest to the stag's head. The material gives a good grip, particularly if the hand is wet when using the knife. Other models had walnut, boxwood, or ash handles or were made of bone, whittled to give the impression that the handle was really made of antler.

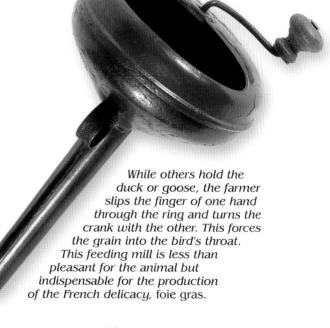

While others hold the duck or goose, the farmer slips the finger of one hand through the ring and turns the crank with the other. This forces the grain into the bird's throat. This feeding mill is less than pleasant for the animal but indispensable for the production of the French delicacy, foie gras.

Pair of secateurs with additional
blade. It has a forged steel handle
fitted with a spur to prevent
the hand from slipping.
This pair doubles as
a small axe, for pruning
vines, for example.

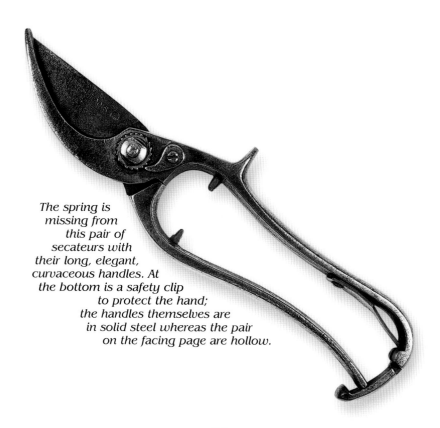

The spring is missing from this pair of secateurs with their long, elegant, curvaceous handles. At the bottom is a safety clip to protect the hand; the handles themselves are in solid steel whereas the pair on the facing page are hollow.

This pair of secateurs is said to be Bordeaux style due to the wavy contour of its upper blade, which gives it an air of solidity. Note the clasp, held in place by a screw, for adjusting the pressure between the two blades and the thumb without the aid of a screwdriver.

A dual-function winegrower's axe. The hooked blade on one side is for pruning, while the hammer on the other side drives in the stakes that support the vine.

In his remarkable work on edge tools, Daniel Boucard shows a special pruning tool used for cutting the branches of mulberry bushes, the favorite food of the Bombyx larva, otherwise known as the silkworm. The Goldenberg catalog of 1927 also features just such a specialized implement. This model has two blades that have been well worn by use.

This tool is considered to be one
of the most dangerous to use.
It is a hoof parer or farrier's gouge,
used to trim the sole of horses' hooves
before fitting the horseshoe.
In old catalogs, this tool
came in all kinds of
models from all over
Europe—France, Spain,
Austria, Hungary.

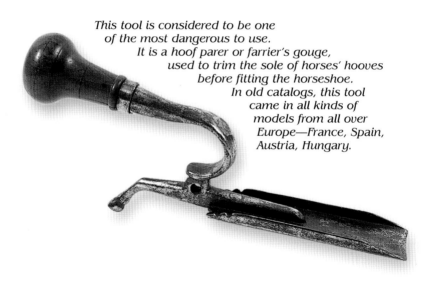

The farrier's hammer,
used for hammering
in the nails that pin
the shoe to the
horse's hoof.
Its front
peen is
split.

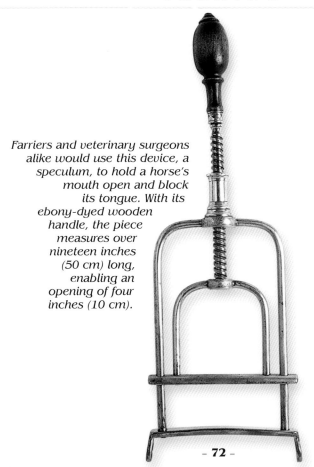

Farriers and veterinary surgeons alike would use this device, a speculum, to hold a horse's mouth open and block its tongue. With its ebony-dyed wooden handle, the piece measures over nineteen inches (50 cm) long, enabling an opening of four inches (10 cm).

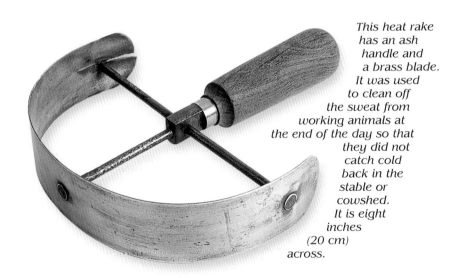

This heat rake has an ash handle and a brass blade. It was used to clean off the sweat from working animals at the end of the day so that they did not catch cold back in the stable or cowshed. It is eight inches (20 cm) across.

There are several models of farriers' tail dockers. The blacksmith needed a wide range of implements and tools, as his job often overlapped with that of the veterinary surgeon.

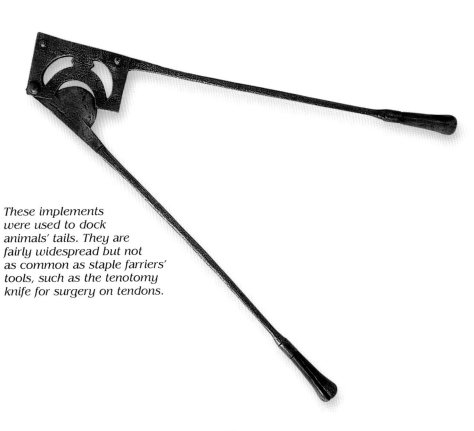

These implements were used to dock animals' tails. They are fairly widespread but not as common as staple farriers' tools, such as the tenotomy knife for surgery on tendons.

These implements were generally used by veterinary surgeons for minor operations on animals. Farriers or livestock owners might also own one, along with the farrier's knife.

This tool is made entirely of steel to give it added weight. It is an early tooth breaker, made for breaking horse's teeth when fitting a bit. The tooth in question was inserted in the hollow end of the tool. The sliding tube over the shaft was pushed forcefully toward the tooth and crack! Ouch!

*These
primitive shears
go back to the
earliest times. Used in
the past for cutting fabric
and tinplate and shearing sheep,
the design is popular today
among holistic gardeners
for light duty urban
gardening.*

This is a variation on the shears on the facing page. This hand-held pair of sheep-shears is similar to the 1926 Peugeot catalog model "La Rapide," designed for use on dogs and sheep. The brand name, Delta, is marked on the side. Note the crisscross-embossed thumb support, for right-handers. The principle is straightforward—there is one mobile cutting blade and six supporting teeth.

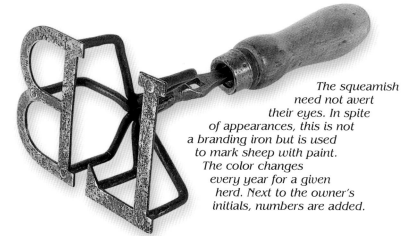

The squeamish
need not avert
their eyes. In spite
of appearances, this is not
a branding iron but is used
to mark sheep with paint.
The color changes
every year for a given
herd. Next to the owner's
initials, numbers are added.

This is a pair of
hedge-clippers.
They come in all
shapes and sizes,
according to preference.
Using them takes some
effort: the handles of this pair
are set at an angle to the blades
to protect the hands and also
ease the back when
snipping low greenery.

*This receptacle, worn
by reapers who attached
them to their belts, contained
a whetstone. This model, is made
of wood; others were made of ox horn or sheet metal.
To retain moisture, they were filled with grass and water.*

This is a crescent-shaped pruning hook. The blade was fitted to a long handle and used to prune the high branches of trees and hedges.

This beautifully-made skimmer is carved from a single piece of beech and was used to skim the cream from milk. The piece dates from the middle of the nineteenth century.

Butter molds were generally carved from maple or lime, woods that are easy to work as they have practically no grain.

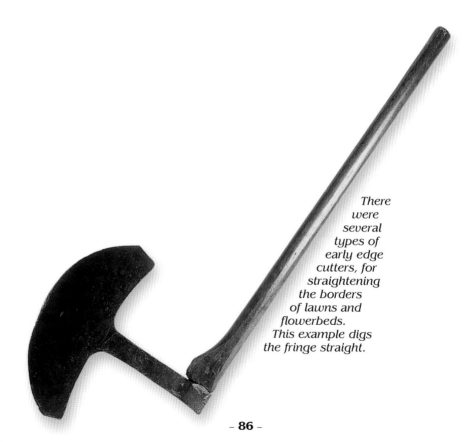

There were several types of early edge cutters, for straightening the borders of lawns and flowerbeds. This example digs the fringe straight.

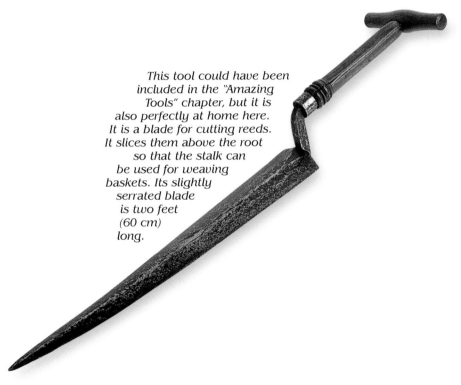

This tool could have been included in the "Amazing Tools" chapter, but it is also perfectly at home here. It is a blade for cutting reeds. It slices them above the root so that the stalk can be used for weaving baskets. Its slightly serrated blade is two feet (60 cm) long.

Even if it is made of wood, a shovel is always a shovel. This piece is still in good condition and must have been mainly used in soft, loose soil. Its blade is reinforced with a metal plate which no doubt helped to preserve it.

The British have always produced high-quality tools. This straight-edged spade is made by Eckardts, in their "Ideal" range, and dates from the 1930s.

The small plaque on the handle announces that this model is a multi-use pair of "Astor Shears for hedges and grass," obviously made in England. This solid piece has a nine-inch (23 cm) cutting width.

This type of hoe was used by well diggers. The ribs help clayey soil to slide off more easily than it does from a smooth blade. Note the wooden wedge that holds the blade onto the handle.

Flails are
straightforward
tools with interesting
variations in detail depending
on their function. This model, with its
flat thresher paddle, was used for threshing
beans in the Arpajon area to the south of Paris,
which was famous for this particular vegetable. The
model on the facing page, with its hardwood cylindrical
beater, was used more or less all over France...

... for threshing wheat
and other cereal crops.
Note the marvelous leather
straps connecting the handle
to the beater. In some regions,
these hinges were made from
the skins of vipers.

This blade is used to tap the resin from pine trees. Once driven into the trunk, it supports the bucket that collects the resin...

... but first the tapper uses this axe to cut a vertical hole in the bark out of which the resin flows.

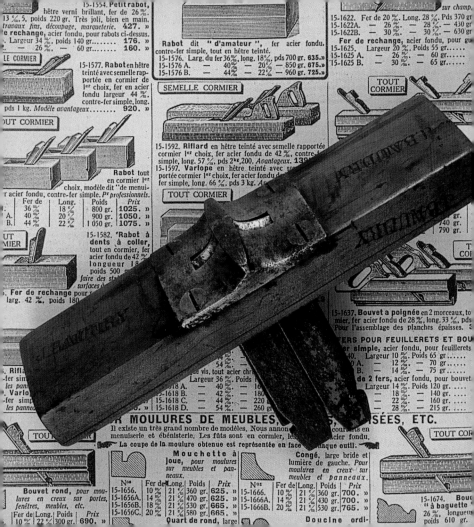

15-1554. Petit rabot, hêtre verni brillant, fer de 26 ⅜. travaux fins, découpage, marqueterie. **427. »**
e de rechange, acier fondu, pour rabots ci-dessus.
. Largeur 34 ⅜.. poids 140 gr...... **176. »**
— 26 ⅜ — 60 gr........ **160. »**

LE CORMIER

15-1577. Rabot en hêtre teinté avec semelle rapportée en cormier de 1er choix, fer en acier fondu largeur 44 ⅜. contre-fer simple, long. pds 1 kg. Modèle avantageux. **920. »**

OUT CORMIER

Rabot tout en cormier 1er choix, modèle dit "de menui-r acier fondu, contre-fer simple. Pt professionnels.

Fer de	Long.	Poids	Prix
36 ⅜	18 ⅜	800 gr.	1025. »
A. 40 ⅜	20 ⅜	900 gr.	1050. »
B. 44 ⅜	22 ⅜	1 050 gr.	1075. »

Fer de rechange pour
larg. 42 ⅜. poids 180

15-1582. 'Rabot à dents à coller, tout en cormier, fer acier fondu de 42 ⅜ longueur 18 poids 560 faire des st surfaces col

. Rifla les pann . Varlo les panne

Rabot dit "**d'amateur**", fer acier fondu, contre-fer simple, tout en hêtre teinté.
15-1576. Larg. du fer 36⅜, long. 15⅜. pds 700 gr. **635. »**
15-1576 A. — 40⅜ — 20⅜ — 850 gr. **675. »**
15-1576 B. — 44⅜ — 22⅜ — 960 gr. **725. »**

SEMELLE CORMIER

15-1592. Riflard en hêtre teinté avec semelle rapportée cormier 1er choix, fer acier fondu de 42 ⅜, contre-simple, long. 57 ⅜. pds 2kg.200. Avantageux. **139**
15-1597. Varlope en hêtre teinté avec sem portée cormier 1er choix, fer acier fondu de se fer simple, long. 66 ⅜. pds 3 kg. 1

TOUT CORMIER

---

sur champ.
15-1622. Fer de 20 ⅜. Long. 28 ⅜. Pds 370 gr.
15-1622A. — 26 ⅜ — 28 ⅜ — 430 gr.
15-1622B. — 30 ⅜ — 30 ⅜ — 430 gr.
Fer de rechange, acier fondu, pour gu
15-1625. Largeur 20 ⅜. Poids 55 gr.
15-1625 A. — 26 ⅜ — 60 gr.
15-1625 B. — 30 ⅜ — 65 gr.

TOUT CORMIER

gr.
740 gr.
790 gr.

15-1637. Bouvet à poignée en 2 morceaux, mier, fer acier fondu de 28 ⅜, long. 33 ⅜. pds Pour l'assemblage des planches épaisses.

ERS POUR FEUILLERETS ET BOU
simple, acier fondu, pour feuillerets
Largeur 10 ⅜. Poids 65 gr.
0 A. — 12 ⅜ — 70 gr.
0 B. — 14 ⅜ — 75 gr.
de 2 fers, acier fondu, pour bouvet
Largeur 14 ⅜. Poids 120 gr.
18 ⅜ — 140 gr.
22 ⅜ — 160 gr.
28 ⅜ — 215 gr.

à vis, tout acier chr
— 54 ⅜
Largeur 36 ⅜. Poids
15-1618 A. — 40 ⅜
15-1618 B. — 42 ⅜
15-1618 C. — 44 ⅜
15-1618 D. — 54 ⅜

R MOULURES DE MEUBLES ..., ...SÉES, ETC.
Il existe un très grand nombre de modèles. Nous annon ...cou...ts en menuiserie et ébénisterie. Les fûts sont en cormier, les ...acier fondu.
La coupe de la moulure obtenue est représentée en face ...aque outil.

Mouchette à Joue, pour moulures sur meubles et panneaux.

Congé, large bride et lumière de gauche. Pour moulures en creux sur meubles et panneaux.

Nos	Fer de	Long.	Poids	Prix
15-1656.	10 ⅜	21 ⅜	360 gr.	625. »
15-1656A.	14 ⅜	21 ⅜	470 gr.	625. »
15-1656B.	18 ⅜	21 ⅜	530 gr.	665. »
15-1656C.	20 ⅜	21 ⅜	580 gr.	665. »

Nos	Fer de	Long.	Poids	Prix
15-1666.	10 ⅜	21 ⅜	360 gr.	700. »
15-1666A.	14 ⅜	21 ⅜	430 gr.	700. »
15-1666B.	18 ⅜	21 ⅜	530 gr.	765. »

Bouvet rond, pour moulures en creux sur portes, fenêtres, meubles, etc.

Fer de	Long.	Poids	Prix
22 ⅜	300 gr.	690. »

Quart de rond, large
Doucine ordi-

15-1674. Bou à baguette 26 ⅜, longueu poids 610

II

WOODWORKING
hand tools

Wood is perhaps the most widely available of all construction materials. It is also the least expensive, which explains the great variety of tools developed to work it. Wood needs to be chopped down, cut up, and squared. Some sections need to be removed, others inserted. It needs to be drilled, tapped, planed and carved with the aid of paring chisels, rabbet planes, trying planes, molding planes, etc. The variety of planes alone is immense, their uses just as diverse. As long as there is enough space at home for them, the enthusiastic collector can forage happily in flea markets for ever more specimens.

*Woodcutters
use these axes
to mark trees for felling. They remove the
bark at foot and head height with the blade,
then use the hammer end to imprint their mark
or initials. Once cut down, the stump and trunk
retain their signature.*

The woodcutter who owned the axe on the facing page filed off the initials to prevent anyone else from using them after he retired. On the axe on this page, the initials DL still stand out visibly. Note the slit at the side to let the wood shavings fall away easily.

This implement, a cross between a chisel and an axe, is a carpenter's mortising axe. At one end is a chisel, at the other a mortise chisel. This type, with its boxwood handle, was commonly used in the Languedoc region. This one was made by S. Mora.

This is another type of mortising axe, also used by carpenters. One just like it is illustrated in Guillaume Caoursin's history of the 1480 siege of Rhodes, written in 1490.

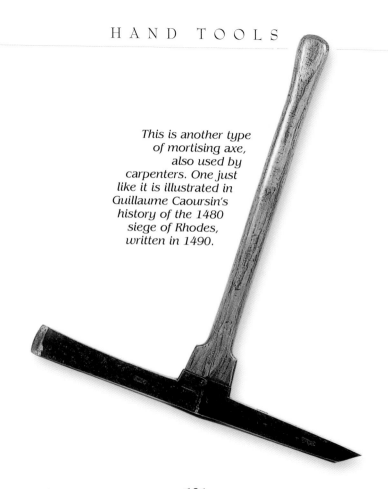

Another long mortising axe, a version of the same tool featured on page 100. This model measures almost four feet (115 cm) long and has a wooden handle. It is made of five sections of steel soldered together and, according to museum curator Daniel Lesoimier, it is probably from Normandy in the north of France.

*This sickle chisel is used
by carpenters for repairs.
It is operated with one hand,
which is practical when standing
on a rickety ladder, perched thirty feet
off the ground. This particular
tool may come from
the Alsace-Lorraine region
in the east of France.*

All Mediterranean countries use stirrup adzes such as these, a tradition that goes back thousands of years. This model is Spanish. Note the steel cutting scoop, as well as the marvelous five-crown logo surrounding the manufacturer's name.

This cooper's adze, signed J. Ayrollec, Paris, is a paring tool. The cooper's adze often has a head on one side and a blade on the other.

These handsome axes were not made for felling trees but for shaping the felled trunks. They serve to dress wood by stripping the trunk to the right dimension through repeated hacking. This task could be carried out directly in the forest after felling, or later at the workshop.

Note the long casing for the handle as well as the large cutting edge ground with a double bevel, so that the carpenter could work toward the left or right. Adroit handling by skilled craftsmen turned felled tree-trunks into smooth beams with precise dimensions.

This small axe was used by joiners and carpenters alike to rough-hew wooden planks or beams into shape before using more precise tools to carve and smooth. This model dates from the eighteenth century. The plane of the blade forms an angle with the handle.

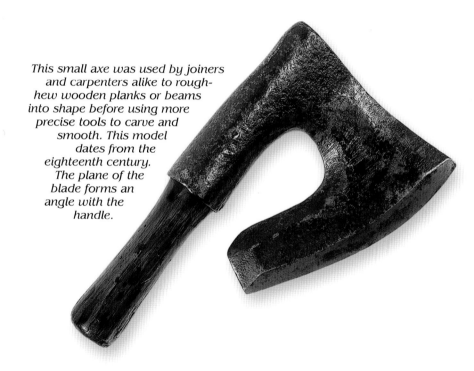

This carpenter's axe is stronger and heavier than the model on the facing page. It was wielded in one hand and was used to square wood. It probably dates from the fourteenth century, to judge from the shape of the handle casing.

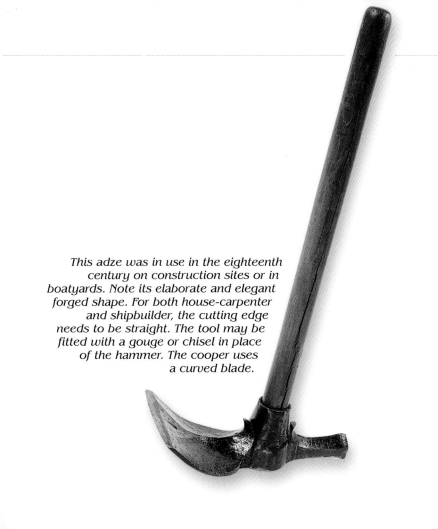

This adze was in use in the eighteenth century on construction sites or in boatyards. Note its elaborate and elegant forged shape. For both house-carpenter and shipbuilder, the cutting edge needs to be straight. The tool may be fitted with a gouge or chisel in place of the hammer. The cooper uses a curved blade.

This adze with its characteristic stirrup is of Mediterranean origin. It was used with both hands, to pare beams on the construction site or in the boatyard. The oak handle is a recent addition but it is crafted in the same style as models from the start of the nineteenth century, the period when this adze was certainly forged.

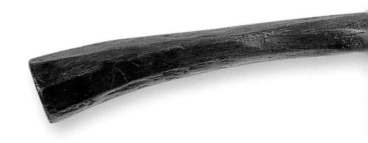

This implement dates from the eighteenth century and has three salient features: a double cutting edge, one along the blade and the other at the head; a geometric design; and a handle at an angle to the axis to protect the hand. It was used by coopers for notching wood. The Goldenberg catalog of 1927 features a similar model.

Like the small carpenters' axes on page 109, this model is used one-handed. The end of the handle has its unusually wide shape because it rests against the cooper or stave-maker's hip. The stave-maker worked for the joiner from whom he would acquire knot-free, fine-grained wood. This superb piece dates from the seventeenth century.

This tool may resemble a pick but was actually used in barrel making. The stave-maker would use it to cut his staves. It is used with the handle upright and blade below, in a swinging vertical movement to splice planks.

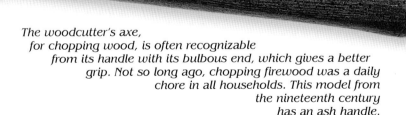

The woodcutter's axe, for chopping wood, is often recognizable from its handle with its bulbous end, which gives a better grip. Not so long ago, chopping firewood was a daily chore in all households. This model from the nineteenth century has an ash handle.

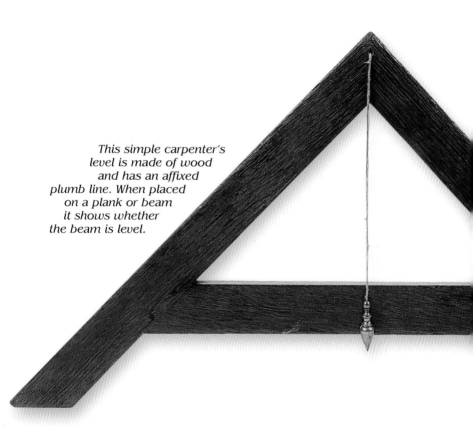

This simple carpenter's level is made of wood and has an affixed plumb line. When placed on a plank or beam it shows whether the beam is level.

The French name for the folding rule is a "pied de roi," or "royal foot," so called because the foot (32.4 cm) is said to have been introduced as a standard measure by the Emperor Charlemagne in the eighth century. This one is signed Delamarre, Paris, and dates from the eighteenth century.

Measure twice, cut once. This type of folding rule is so widespread that a special pocket is sewn into carpenters' pants for it. Whether calibrated in inches or centimeters, or made of wood, steel or aluminum, this tool is basic and universal.

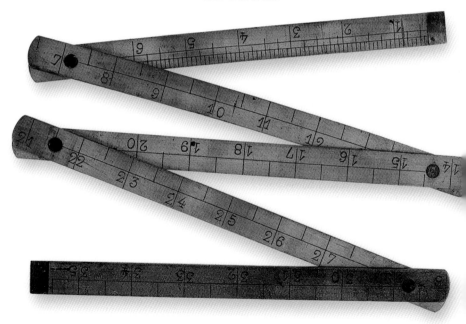

The bevel is used
to measure angles. This
one is made of wood but they
also come in iron, brass, and
aluminum, among other materials.
There are also T-shaped bevels
with a folding cross bar.

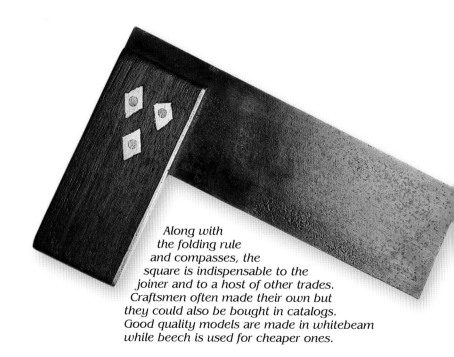

Along with
the folding rule
and compasses, the
square is indispensable to the
joiner and to a host of other trades.
Craftsmen often made their own but
they could also be bought in catalogs.
Good quality models are made in whitebeam
while beech is used for cheaper ones.

This wooden cooper's compass comes from the Burgundy region. It was used to mark the divisions of the staves and trace out the circumference of the barrel head. The two points diverge or converge when the horizontal rod, with its inverted threads, is turned. This model dates from the nineteenth century.

A groove inserted in door or
window frames for the
insertion of glass is called
a rabbet. To produce a
rabbet, a long rabbet
plane is needed and the
longer it is, the straighter
the rabbet will be. At the
Musée d'Outil ancien,
there is an example of a
rabbet plane, dated 1823,
measuring four feet (120 cm) long.

A plane used to make dowel pins or to level off wooden rods or handles. The wood is shaped roughly to size then introduced into the upper hole. The two handles serve to turn the plane. Also called a rounding plane.

The blade is angled so as to emerge almost at the front edge of this plane. It is used to plane as closely as possible into corners.

This attractively crafted brass plane was designed for finishing. The angle of its blade allows it to shave off very thin layers of wood. It dates from the nineteenth century.

This attractive marking gauge with two guides has an acorn-shaped knob that is as useful for handling as it is decorative. It dates from the nineteenth century and may have been used by a cabinet-maker for veneering work.

Another rabbet plane. The tip of the blade is positioned far forward, allowing it to remove excess wood even in corners. The large screw is used to hold the blade in place.

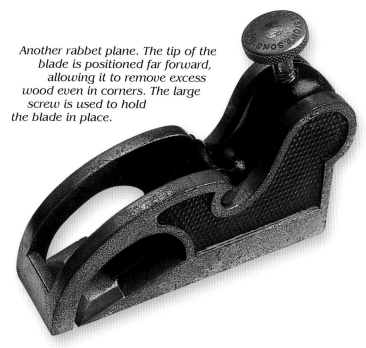

*This router plane is a smaller member of the plane
family and is used for smoothing hollows and
recesses. It is generally made of whitebeam, but
this Stanley model,
from the 1950s,
is metal.*

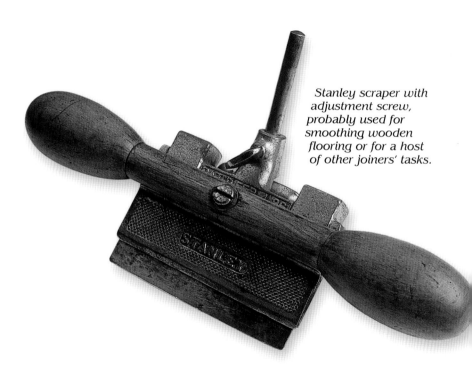

Stanley scraper with adjustment screw, probably used for smoothing wooden flooring or for a host of other joiners' tasks.

*The "Floor-Scrapers" in the famous
1875 painting by Gustave Caillebotte
might well have been using scrapers
like these. The painting gives a good
idea of just how painful it must
have been to work with this
tool, day in, day out.*

This Stanley 45 multi-plane dates from the middle of the twentieth century. It can be fitted with fifty or more different blades, allowing it to be used as a shoulder, rabbet, plow, or molding plane. The Stanley Tool Company, the American tool brand, was founded at the end of the nineteenth century and had a huge manufacturing base in Roxton Pond, Canada, between 1907 and 1984.

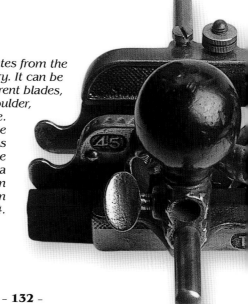

The jack plane is a large plane for removing the warping in wood and smoothing its rough edges. For finishing, finer planes are used. The Goldenberg catalog of 1927 features a number of jack planes: the cheapest are made of beech or hornbeam; the middle range is made of fruitwood; the top range in whitebeam or green oak.

This is a match plane, or tongue and groove plane, used, as the names suggest, to carve out matching tongues and grooves in wood. Its blades are generally narrow and it has a guide runner on one side. This model is operated with both hands and has two blades, directed both ways, for dual action planing, one blade producing the tongue, the other the groove. Note the blade in the middle of the plane and the guide underneath for precision work.

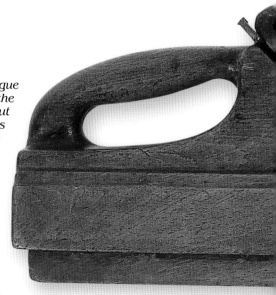

The trying plane is a long joiner's or carpenter's plane used for straightening wood after the rough edges have been removed by a jack plane. This superb piece from the eighteenth century is part of the Bièvres tool museum collection. Its reverse blade is missing here.

Routers
come in all
kinds of shapes. This
tool is often used to
produce adventurous,
complicated forms. A router may be made
for a specific use, intended for just
one piece of furniture.

Craftsmen used to specialize in banister production. The router was an essential implement in their work as it is capable of cutting a groove along a straight or curved surface, so as to insert a contrasting panel of brass or wood. The router is also essential to the cabinetmaker's craft.

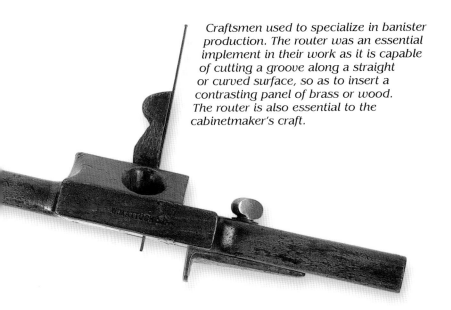

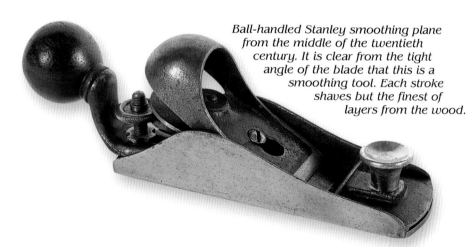

Ball-handled Stanley smoothing plane
from the middle of the twentieth
century. It is clear from the tight
angle of the blade that this is a
smoothing tool. Each stroke
shaves but the finest of
layers from the wood.

This plane with its adjustable base was conceived to smooth curved surfaces. The original shown here was made by Stanley but other manufacturers also had models on sale in the middle of the last century. The screw-wheel on the left adjusts the depth of the curve of the base.

This plane has a sturdy handle at the front for both solid grip and ornament. This ornate model with its detachable sole probably dates from the start of the nineteenth century. It has a hardwood body and the iron is locked onto the blade bed by a wooden wedge.

This object is a trompe-l'oeil invention. It may look like a plane, but it is in fact a snuff-box with a pivoting lid.

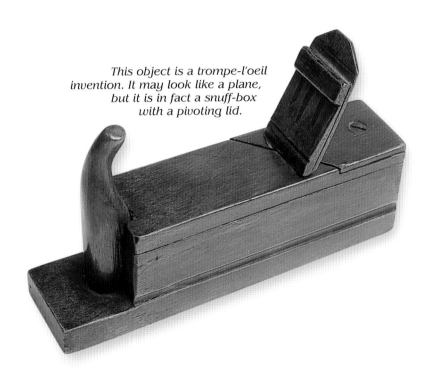

A croze is the name given both to an adjustable tool fitted with a narrow blade and to the recesses that it cuts, that is to say, the two interior grooves in the staves into which barrel heads are fitted. The croze comes in other forms...

*...including
one with a curved base. A
variety of models feature in the 1927
catalog of the great edge-tool maker,
Goldenberg, based in Zornhoff in Alsace.
These pieces were made of beech, hornbeam,
fruitwood, or whitebeam, in increasing order of quality.*

This edge plane was used to work the edges of wooden panels so as to slot them into a frame securely on all four sides, such as when making panels for doors. Note the scoring blade at the front.

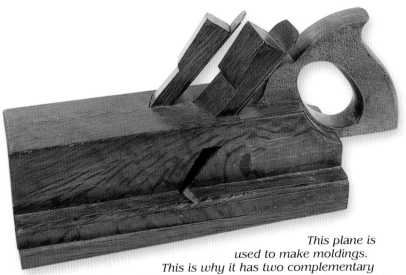

*This plane is
used to make moldings.
This is why it has two complementary
blades, slightly out of kilter to each other, that work in
tandem. The attractive, high-quality molding plane is made of green oak.*

This large plane is carved from a single piece of wood and was used for paring planks for wooden flooring. This particular tool requires four hands for operation. One craftsman takes the handles at the rear to push the implement and press it against the surface of the wood, while another takes the front handles and pulls them, sometimes using a strap to make the task less strenuous.

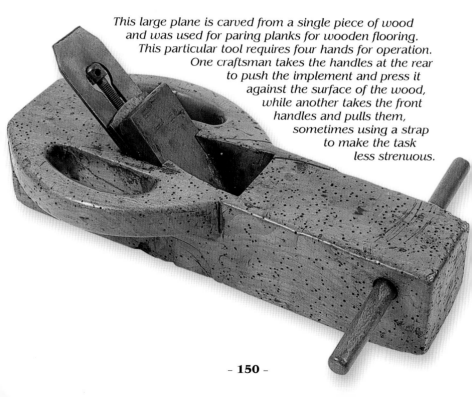

Tools in general, and this wheelwright's rabbet plane in particular, were often marked with the name of their retailer— "Au Marteau d'or, Jean Boyau, 164, boulevard Pereire, à Paris"— as well as that of their owner, here a certain A. Bouche.

Wheelwright's squirrel tail plane, nineteenth century. The two handles allow a good grip on the tool while its short sole means it can be used in tight spaces.

The shaft and sole of the wheelwright's rabbet plane came in many different shapes. This model, featuring an engraved heart, has a concave sole.

Planes used by makers of stringed instruments have to be very small to fit tight corners and only shave sparingly. This is why they are called finger planes.

Tiny finger plane made of steel.
The photograph is actual size.
Other models were made of brass,
but the blade was always
made of steel.

Two different perspectives on a cooper's howel, used in the latter stages of barrel production. The staves are provisionally assembled and a croze applied. The howel is then used to smooth the interior edges of the barrel, the chime, to help fit the barrel heads.

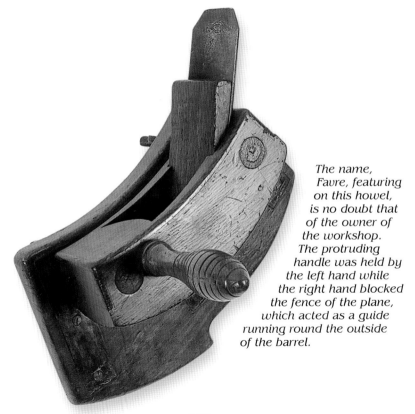

The name,
Favre, featuring
on this howel,
is no doubt that
of the owner of
the workshop.
The protruding
handle was held by
the left hand while
the right hand blocked
the fence of the plane,
which acted as a guide
running round the outside
of the barrel.

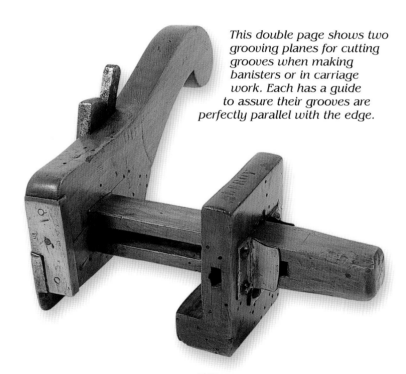

This double page shows two grooving planes for cutting grooves when making banisters or in carriage work. Each has a guide to assure their grooves are perfectly parallel with the edge.

The plane in a carpenter's workshop surprisingly shares the same initial meaning as the plane of "airplane." It was imagined, before an airplane even got off the ground, that its wings and structure would be flat rather than curved and angled.

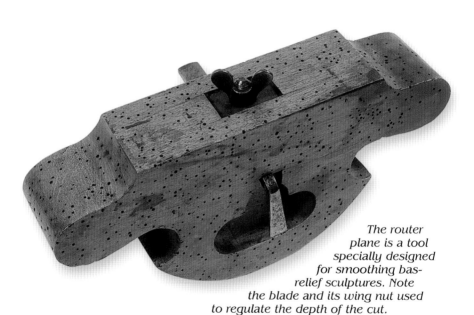

The router plane is a tool specially designed for smoothing bas-relief sculptures. Note the blade and its wing nut used to regulate the depth of the cut.

A wheelwright's grooving plane is instantly recognizable by its short sole. This plane is made of mahogany. The brass plaque is stamped with the name "R. Rochechouart 5."

This small plane is a spokeshave and has two handles and a curved blade used for planing curves. This model is made of mahogany and has a metal sole.

The draw-chisel is used in a number of trades. This carpenter's draw-chisel is used to score the timbers of a house, which are often set up on a trial basis in the workshop. Note the lever fitting at the other end of the blade.

This frame saw, c. 1930, neatly folds away for easy storage. It is a household saw capable of any number of tasks, from shortening a broom handle to cutting up packing cases to feed the kitchen stove.

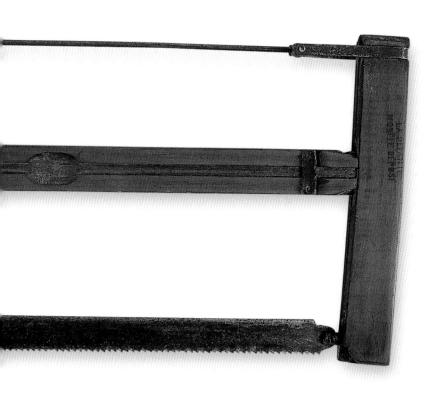

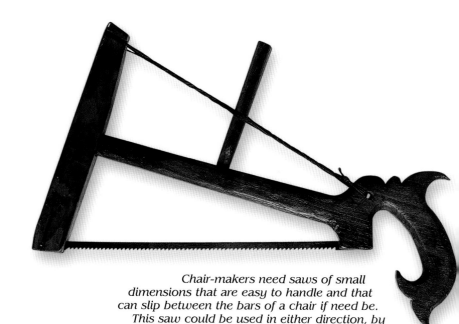

*Chair-makers need saws of small
dimensions that are easy to handle and that
can slip between the bars of a chair if need be.
This saw could be used in either direction, by
holding the handle end or its opposite.*

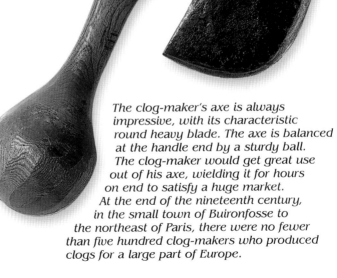

The clog-maker's axe is always
impressive, with its characteristic
round heavy blade. The axe is balanced
at the handle end by a sturdy ball.
The clog-maker would get great use
out of his axe, wielding it for hours
on end to satisfy a huge market.
At the end of the nineteenth century,
in the small town of Buironfosse to
the northeast of Paris, there were no fewer
than five hundred clog-makers who produced
clogs for a large part of Europe.

To carve white poplar, a commonly used wood in clog-making, very sharp tools were necessary. This clog-maker's paring blade is three feet (90 cm) long and was fixed to the work block by the hook at the end. It was used to shape the exterior of the clog.

The clog-maker would use this hook-tipped gouge to smooth the inside of the clog, paring away the finest of wood shavings for the better comfort of our forefathers' feet. The clog-maker would always make two clogs at once to make sure they matched as a pair.

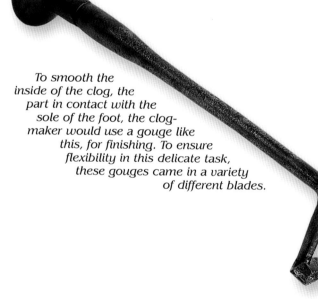

*To smooth the
inside of the clog, the
part in contact with the
sole of the foot, the clog-
maker would use a gouge like
this, for finishing. To ensure
flexibility in this delicate task,
these gouges came in a variety
of different blades.*

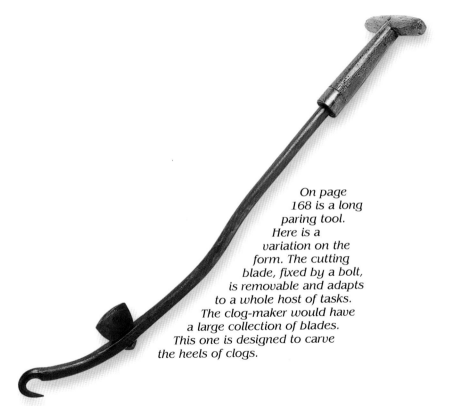

On page
168 is a long
paring tool.
Here is a
variation on the
form. The cutting
blade, fixed by a bolt,
is removable and adapts
to a whole host of tasks.
The clog-maker would have
a large collection of blades.
This one is designed to carve
the heels of clogs.

*This keyhole saw is, as its name suggests,
narrow enough to slip through a small hole
and then cut apertures of any size and shape.
The saw shown at the top of the page is
a basic garden saw, of which there are several
models in the 1926 Peugeot catalog.
The handles on both are particularly elegant.*

This odd-looking short saw with two handles is a dado saw. It was used with a ruler to score wood in marquetry and cut the dados for stair treads.

Like the model on the facing page, this saw with two handles is also a dado saw.

Drawknife used to split chestnut saplings to obtain the hooping for Burgundy style barrels. This superb example is marked "Cornelius Whitehouse & Sons—Cannock" and "Hedgehog Reg. Trademark." Markings like these may also add value to a tool.

This hooped drawknife is a cooper's tool, used to smooth the inside of a barrel, tun or cask. In 1899, Peugeot had a range of both hooped and curved drawknives, in fifteen different lengths of blade from eight to almost twenty inches (20 to 50 cm).

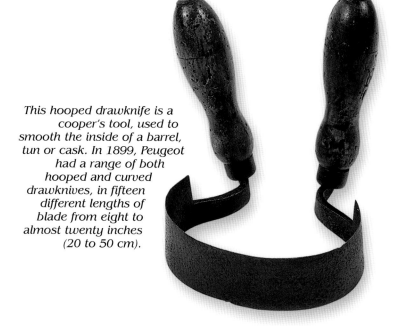

The cooper's dog,
made of wood with
an iron-capped tip and
a hinged blade, is used to
spread the staves to fit the
barrel bottom. The curved blade
holds the top of the stave while
the tip grips the hooping of the barrel.

This hooked
gouge was once a
tool used by tax officers to
mark wine casks. Over the years
it became a cooper's tool, used for the
same function. The central spike is a pivot
for the curved blade which gouges rings. The
angled double-edged blade cuts straight lines
and curves. This gouge, stamped with its owner's
initials, measures almost five inches (12 cm).

This woodcutter's gouge is larger than that of the barrel-maker on the facing page. It measures ten inches (25 cm). It is used to mark trunks and was produced by the Blanchard workshop, a manufacturer who will feature again in the leatherworking tools chapter.

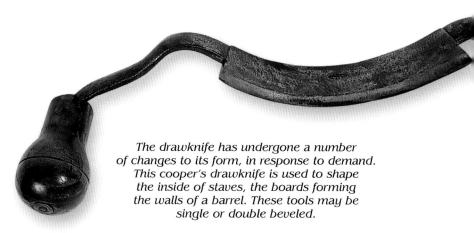

The drawknife has undergone a number of changes to its form, in response to demand. This cooper's drawknife is used to shape the inside of staves, the boards forming the walls of a barrel. These tools may be single or double beveled.

Cooper's
band driver
made of ash, from
the Bordeaux area,
in southwest France.
The end of the handle
and the frame of the blade
are ironclad, reinforced to
withstand being hit by a
hammer. Coopers use this
implement, striking it with a good
heavy hammer to position the metal
hoops that hold and protect the barrel,
hence the ridged blade.

Before electric drills came into being, a huge array of tools were invented to drill through wood, brass, and iron. The mechanism of this pump drill dates back to the dawn of time. People in Asia and Africa still use this type of drill. Up until twenty years ago, it was a part of the clock-makers' and jewelers' toolkit, used for precision drilling.

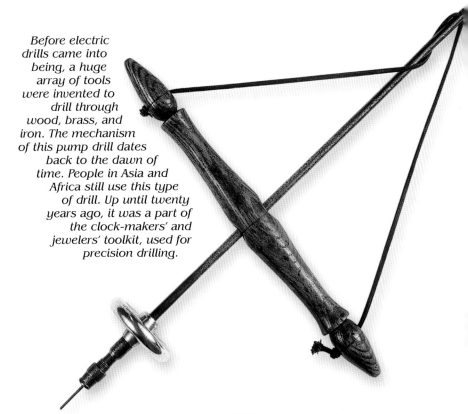

This model was more widespread and works on the pump-drill principle on the facing page. When it comes to boring small holes, it is very precise, but it does have its limits. The tool works by to-and-fro motions and not by continuous drilling.

This mahogany and brass brace is apparently of British origin and dates from the nineteenth century. All kinds of steel and mahogany attachable drill bits were available for drilling and screwing, including those on the facing page. These bits, made of steel and mahogany, were held only by friction in the brace.

There are several kinds of cooper's bores, to make holes for filling and emptying barrels. This model has a spoon bit and a sharp screw point enabling precise positioning of the implement in the barrelhead or staves.

*Another cooper's bore,
this time with a spiral augur bit,
used mainly in the Macon area.
The Champagne region version
of the implement featured
a spoon bit with a rasp
surface. Yet another type
has a conical rasp bit.*

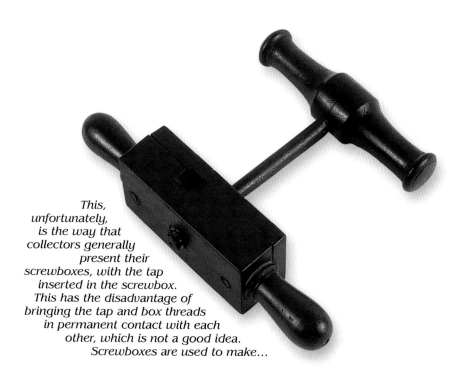

This, unfortunately, is the way that collectors generally present their screwboxes, with the tap inserted in the screwbox. This has the disadvantage of bringing the tap and box threads in permanent contact with each other, which is not a good idea. Screwboxes are used to make...

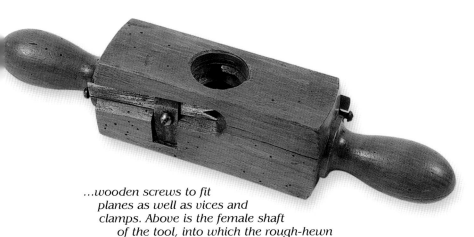

...*wooden screws to fit
planes as well as vices and
clamps. Above is the female shaft
of the tool, into which the rough-hewn
wooden tap is introduced. Walnut, mahogany,
or beech are ideal for such screws.*

These items come from the household rather than the workshop. These twist gimlets are hand drills with a screw tip for easier boring.

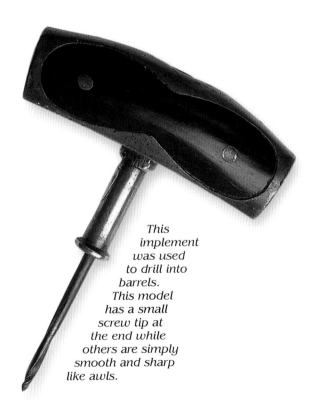

This implement was used to drill into barrels. This model has a small screw tip at the end while others are simply smooth and sharp like awls.

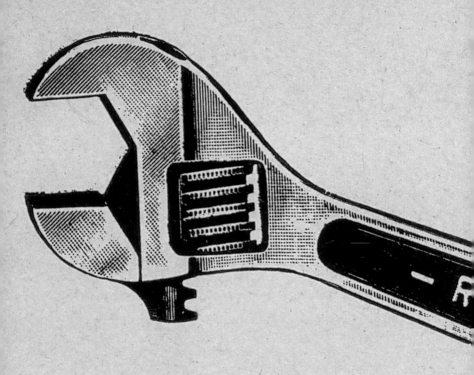

III

METALWORKING
hand tools

Every kind of metal has been used to make tools and to make things with tools. Iron, tin, lead, zinc, silver, gold—only liquid mercury escapes the toolmaker's hand. The value of each metal determines how often it is used to create the tools used by the file-cutter, the nail-maker, the plumber, the tinsmith, the goldsmith, the jeweler, and other craftsmen. Very few metalworking tools are made of wood: at most, wood is adopted as the material for handles.

This gauge rod is one of a whole family of metal tools crafted with all kinds of round, square, rectangular or triangular notches used for measuring thickness and dimensions.

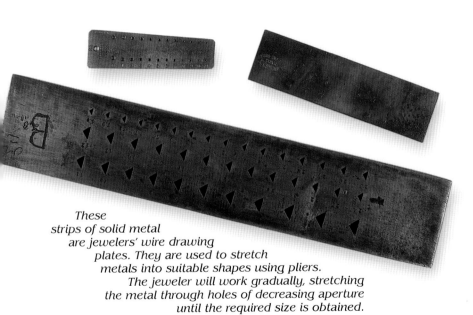

*These
strips of solid metal
are jewelers' wire drawing
plates. They are used to stretch
metals into suitable shapes using pliers.
The jeweler will work gradually, stretching
the metal through holes of decreasing aperture
until the required size is obtained.*

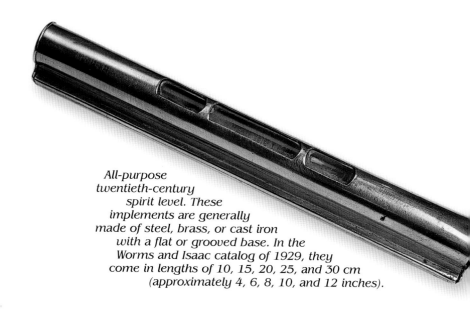

*All-purpose
twentieth-century
spirit level. These
implements are generally
made of steel, brass, or cast iron
with a flat or grooved base. In the
Worms and Isaac catalog of 1929, they
come in lengths of 10, 15, 20, 25, and 30 cm
(approximately 4, 6, 8, 10, and 12 inches).*

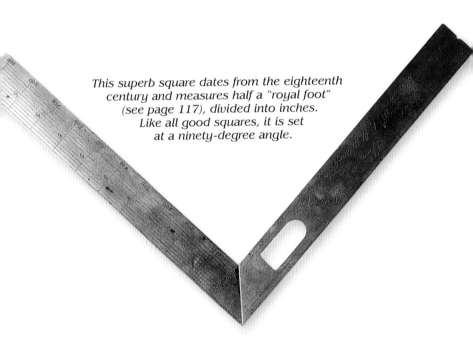

This superb square dates from the eighteenth
century and measures half a "royal foot"
(see page 117), divided into inches.
Like all good squares, it is set
at a ninety-degree angle.

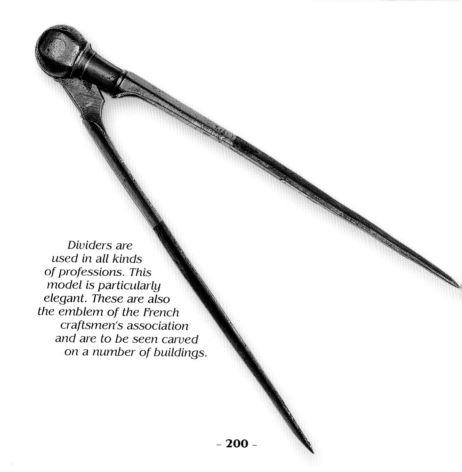

Dividers are used in all kinds of professions. This model is particularly elegant. These are also the emblem of the French craftsmen's association and are to be seen carved on a number of buildings.

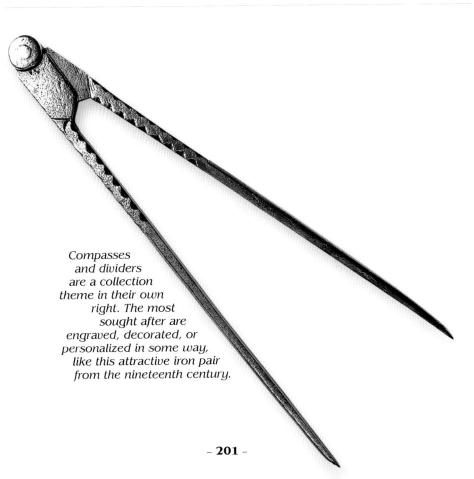

*Compasses
and dividers
are a collection
theme in their own
right. The most
sought after are
engraved, decorated, or
personalized in some way,
like this attractive iron pair
from the nineteenth century.*

This is a set of self-calibrating turners' calipers made of steel. The calibration is set on the quarter-circle runner at the top for opening and closing the implement. In old catalogs these are called "quarter–circle compasses" or "wing compasses."

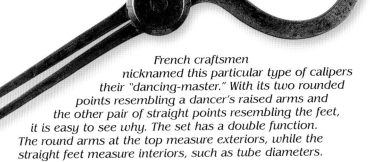

*French craftsmen
nicknamed this particular type of calipers
their "dancing-master." With its two rounded
points resembling a dancer's raised arms and
the other pair of straight points resembling the feet,
it is easy to see why. The set has a double function.
The round arms at the top measure exteriors, while the
straight feet measure interiors, such as tube diameters.*

*A simple pair
of self-adjusting calipers
from the start of the twentieth
century, made of steel and
marked with the initials
of the craftsman
—a turner or a sculptor—
who used them.*

Quarter-circle dividers. The wing nut on the right stem tightens to hold the dividers at a particular angle.

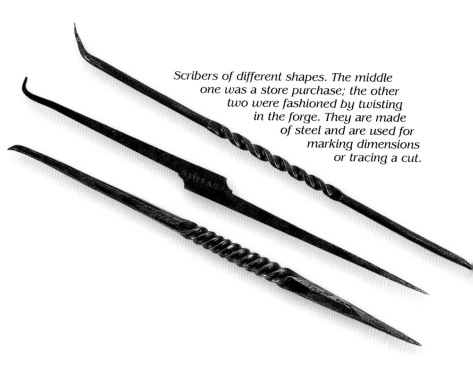

Scribers of different shapes. The middle one was a store purchase; the other two were fashioned by twisting in the forge. They are made of steel and are used for marking dimensions or tracing a cut.

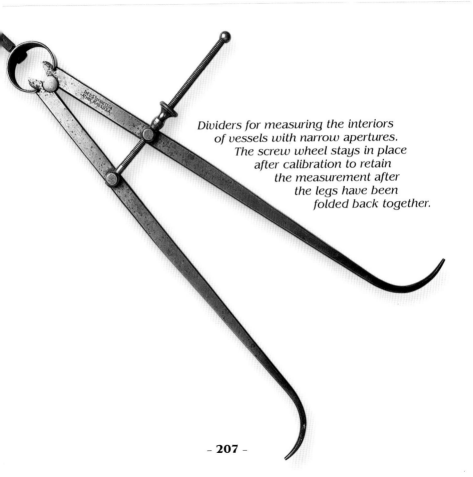

*Dividers for measuring the interiors
of vessels with narrow apertures.
The screw wheel stays in place
after calibration to retain
the measurement after
the legs have been
folded back together.*

This large object is a tinsmith's anvil. It measures one foot, four inches (40 cm) and has several working surfaces, all for shaping sheet metals. Note the two flat edges of differing dimensions on the upper side and the cone for curving surfaces below.

*Spring-loaded
hand-held vice.
By clamping
the lower jaw,
it is possible to fit
the implement to a bench
vice for delicate adjustments
on small pieces. Other hand vices
are equipped with wooden handles.*

This tool is used like a vice clamp for stretching wire or tanned hide or holding assembled parts together. It looks very much like the bookbinder's clamp, but this implement has a wider jaw.

*Aluminum mallet used for working
supple metals that deform
or dent easily but that are
too hard to be treated
with a wooden mallet.*

Upholsterer's hammer, in a Thévenot style, as
described in the catalog of Dandoy-Maillard,
Lucq & Cie, toolmakers since 1816.
Thévenot-style means that the tool
end is attached by a handle casing,
while the usual form has a blind
handle shaft fitted inside the top
third of the handle length.
This hammer is designed
for tacks rather than nails.

*In the days
when small
balls of metal were
homemade, this pair of
lead pincers was essential.
The jaws close on the
metal then open to release
the ball from the mold.*

These two delicate jewelers' hammers are used for the most meticulous of tasks. The handle of the upper hammer is made of wood while that of the lower model is made of dark horn.

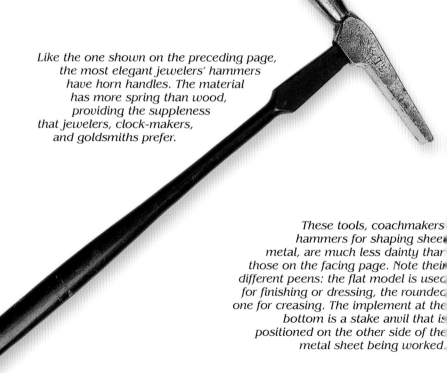

Like the one shown on the preceding page,
the most elegant jewelers' hammers
have horn handles. The material
has more spring than wood,
providing the suppleness
that jewelers, clock-makers,
and goldsmiths prefer.

These tools, coachmakers'
hammers for shaping sheet
metal, are much less dainty than
those on the facing page. Note their
different peens: the flat model is used
for finishing or dressing, the rounded
one for creasing. The implement at the
bottom is a stake anvil that is
positioned on the other side of the
metal sheet being worked.

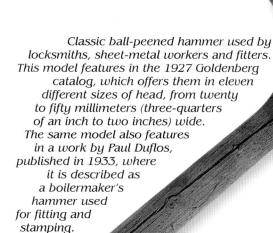

Classic ball-peened hammer used by locksmiths, sheet-metal workers and fitters. This model features in the 1927 Goldenberg catalog, which offers them in eleven different sizes of head, from twenty to fifty millimeters (three-quarters of an inch to two inches) wide. The same model also features in a work by Paul Duflos, published in 1933, where it is described as a boilermaker's hammer used for fitting and stamping.

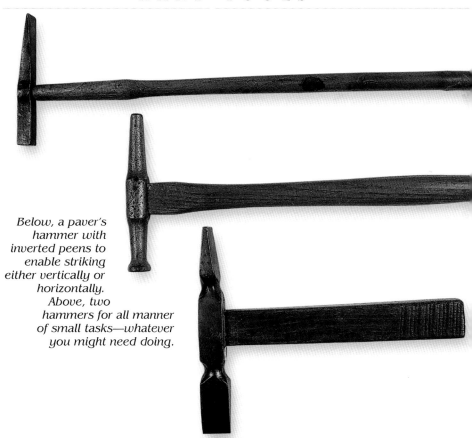

Below, a paver's hammer with inverted peens to enable striking either vertically or horizontally. Above, two hammers for all manner of small tasks—whatever you might need doing.

With its two rounded peens, this hammer belongs in the toolkits of sheet metal workers, tinsmiths or coppersmiths and is used for shaping sheet metal— in particular for rolling and curving tin.

Another hammer from the same toolkit. This one is used for hollowing. With its long peen, it reaches down to the bottom inside edges of iron or copper pots or pitchers.

How many times a minute would this file-cutter's hammer hit its burin? Paul Feller and Fernand Touret, in their book, L' Outil, state that the worker would generally reach eighty to ninety blows a minute with a three-pound hammer, sixty to seventy with a four-pound hammer, and fifty to sixty with their heaviest five-pound implement! And the average working day was ten hours long....

*These different-sized burins were used
by file-cutters to form a succession of parallel
strokes. For rasps, they would use an awl
or punch to cover the iron with tiny teardrops
of metal. Note the wear and tear on the handle
on the facing page, made by the rubbing
of its owner's thumb and forefinger.*

A farrier's maul. This heavy hammer is used to fit the horseshoe to the shape of the horse's hoof. Another type of maul has a wedge-shaped head and is used for splitting logs.

Small handheld vice used for a number of tasks, like making jewelry or flies for trout-fishing. The rather unsightly four-sided nut used to tighten the vice does not appear to be its original, which was probably a wing nut.

*These jewelers' mallets are made of hard boxwood
or steel which, when used in conjunction
with the jewelers' dice on the facing page,
give attractive concave or convex shapes
to silver or gold leaf....*

*...The metal is worked cold. The piece is placed
on one of the dimples of the die and, with the
help of a mallet, the leaf will take shape.
The dice feature dimples of differing widths
to answer all the jeweler's needs.*

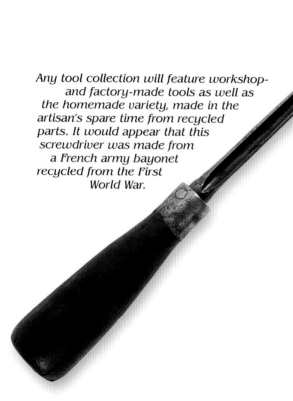

*Any tool collection will feature workshop-
and factory-made tools as well as
the homemade variety, made in the
artisan's spare time from recycled
parts. It would appear that this
screwdriver was made from
a French army bayonet
recycled from the First
World War.*

Engravers and jewelers use burins like these.
The handles are made of turned boxwood or walnut,
the rings of brass and the points of steel.

The gilder
  must be a
    happy man,
  working gold leaf all
    the livelong day. It is a
delicate occupation if ever there was
one—while gold ingots are heavy, gold leaf is
    only a hundred-thousandth of an inch thick.
      It is impossible to pick up by hand so the gilder
        uses a badger-hair brush such as this...

...whose static electricity
keeps the leaf on the brush,
enabling it to be placed wherever
required. The brushes here
have tropical wood handles,
while the badger hairs are glued
to board. On the facing page, there is
a gold-leaf cutter with a walnut handle.

*Burnishers are used in several trades, particularly
by gilders in the bookbinding trade. They are used
to apply gold leaf to the crevices left by the gilding iron.
A mixture of egg white is applied first before working
the leaf into the gaps with the tool.*

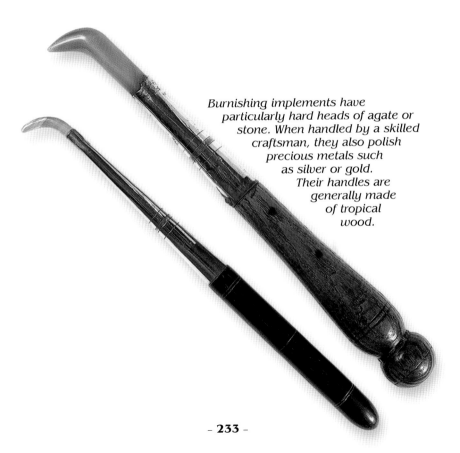

Burnishing implements have particularly hard heads of agate or stone. When handled by a skilled craftsman, they also polish precious metals such as silver or gold. Their handles are generally made of tropical wood.

Tinsnips or shears belonging to tinsmiths or other sheet-metal workers. Depending on the position of the cutting edge, they are called right- or left-handed shears.

Sometimes form overrides questions of function or material, and antique tools look like pieces of sculpture. These shears look a little like a dachshund with its little eye, stumpy legs and tail. This twentieth-century pair has been mounted on a handle to facilitate standardized production work.

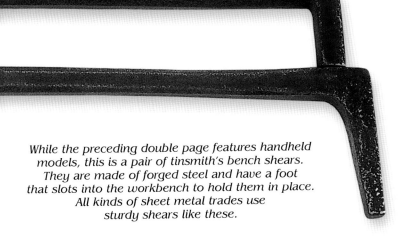

*While the preceding double page features handheld
models, this is a pair of tinsmith's bench shears.
They are made of forged steel and have a foot
that slots into the workbench to hold them in place.
All kinds of sheet metal trades use
sturdy shears like these.*

Bronze spoon mold featuring an insulating wooden handle. The upper section is missing but the funnel for pouring molten pewter is visible on the right.

Pipe cutters used by plumbers to snip sections of lead piping by rotating the jaws around the cylinder and pressing inwards on the cutter's handles.

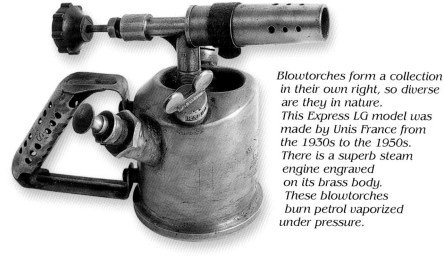

Blowtorches form a collection in their own right, so diverse are they in nature.
This Express LG model was made by Unis France from the 1930s to the 1950s.
There is a superb steam engine engraved on its brass body.
These blowtorches burn petrol vaporized under pressure.

*Blacksmiths would forge their own pliers and pincers,
adapting them for all kinds of specific tasks
and leaving us an abundant supply. Note that
the jaws of these pairs are all different because
each pair is made to clench a different piece
of iron, to hold it firmly in the embers
or beneath hammer blows.*

IV

LEATHERWORKING
hand tools

The cobbler's and saddler's workshops
are permeated above all else with
the aroma of leather. Specialized hand tools
for working that most attractive of materials
are often very beautiful and generally very simple.
In leatherworking, what counts are know-how,
an expert eye, a seasoned hand, and inborn talent.
Anyone who collects and uses such beautiful tools
as round knifes or awls knows how difficult it is to
produce a regular saddle-stitch while simultaneously
gripping the clamp with exactly enough pressure
to hold the work in place.

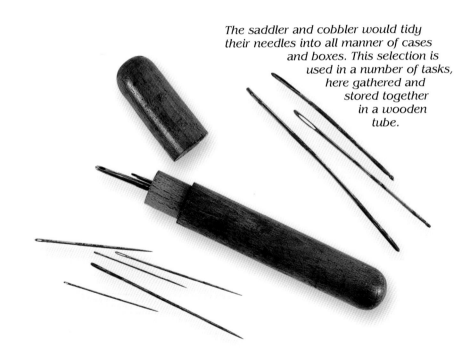

The saddler and cobbler would tidy their needles into all manner of cases and boxes. This selection is used in a number of tasks, here gathered and stored together in a wooden tube.

*Simpler yet just as practical, this strip
of leather fulfills the same function
as the box on the facing page.
Here saddlers' needles are mixed
in with curved upholsterers' needles
and larger packers' needles.*

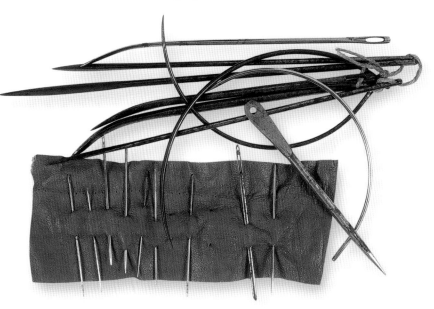

*Saddlers'
knives made
by Blanchard, a
famous French
manufacturer who turned
leatherworking tools into
a specialty. Their small factory,
near Rouen in the north of France,
is still operational. Today handles
are often made of ABS. This older
model has an ebony handle.*

A collection
of very sharp
and slender blades
used to slice leather.
Knives like these featured
in Diderot and d'Alembert's
Grande Encyclopédie in the
eighteenth century. This set
belonged to Émile-Ferdinand Moulin,
a saddler in Houdan, left behind when
he set out for World War I. Sadly,
he never returned to use them again.

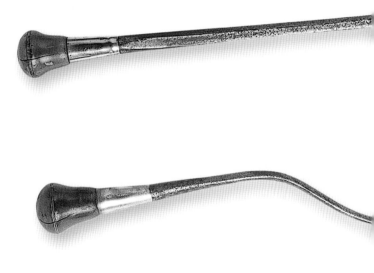

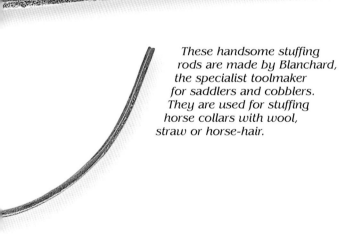

*These handsome stuffing
rods are made by Blanchard,
the specialist toolmaker
for saddlers and cobblers.
They are used for stuffing
horse collars with wool,
straw or horse-hair.*

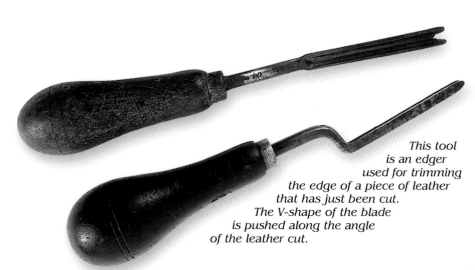

*This tool
is an edger
used for trimming
the edge of a piece of leather
that has just been cut.
The V-shape of the blade
is pushed along the angle
of the leather cut.*

This smoothing iron was used by cobblers to smooth the edges of soles on shoes. These irons often have burn marks on the handle because they were heated on a small stove before being used.

Saddlers' scraper,
also used in other
leatherwork trades.
This tool cuts grooves
in the thickest
of leathers.

*These
slitters or nippers, marked
with the name C. Scelles, are used to cut slits
for belt straps. A model like it features in the 1927
Goldenberg catalog alongside some of its relations,
like buttonhole or shoelace-hole slitters.*

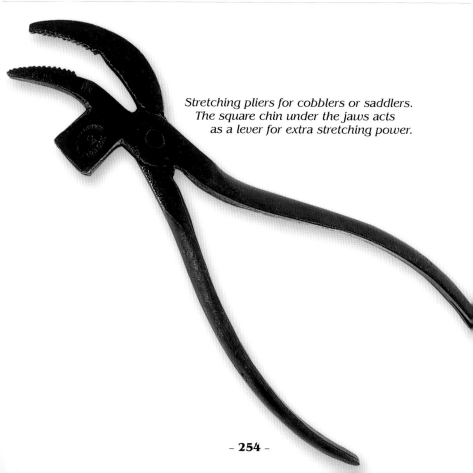

Stretching pliers for cobblers or saddlers. The square chin under the jaws acts as a lever for extra stretching power.

A variation on stretching pliers, boot-makers' mounting pliers for folding the leather under the upper sole before nailing it in place.

*Half-
moon round
knife used
in nearly all
leatherworking trades for
shaving and thinning leather.
It has become the emblem
of the saddlemakers' trade.
Its blade is always
very fine and
extremely
sharp.*

A variation on the form of the saddler's round knife. The model on the right has a tang inserted into the handle. The blade here is mounted using rivets.

In Diderot and d'Alembert's famous encyclopedia, this round knife features i the saddlers' chapter alongside a whole host of tools that have not changed since that superb reference book was published.

The glove-maker's paring knife is exactly like that used in other leatherworking trades. It is used to reduce the thickness of leather to prepare it for stitching or overlays. Bookbinders use the same type of knife. The Rougier & Plé catalog of 1931 features paring knives made of steel four or five and a half inches (110 or 140 mm) long by one and three-quarters or two inches (44 or 50 mm) wide.

Leatherworking uses a great many different hole punches for removing material. The punch may be round, oval or square, and each has a specific application, such as for fitting loops and strap ends (see page 268). The facing page features oblong hole punches, this page features round punches.

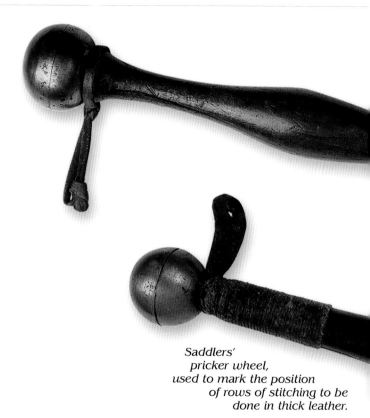

*Saddlers'
pricker wheel,
used to mark the position
of rows of stitching to be
done in thick leather.*

The brass balls at the top of these wheels have two uses: first, they can be unscrewed to store a set of wheels of different shapes and patterns. They also support the shoulder when the tool is being used, so that the teeth of the wheel really sink into the leather.

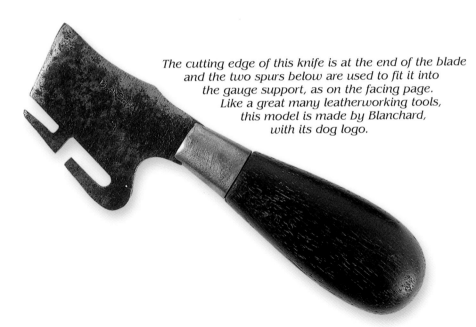

The cutting edge of this knife is at the end of the blade
and the two spurs below are used to fit it into
the gauge support, as on the facing page.
Like a great many leatherworking tools,
this model is made by Blanchard,
with its dog logo.

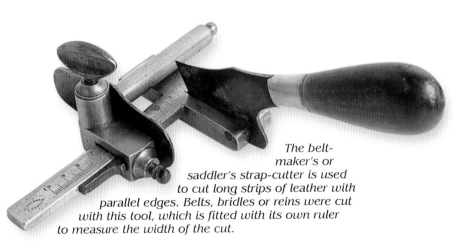

The belt-maker's or saddler's strap-cutter is used to cut long strips of leather with parallel edges. Belts, bridles or reins were cut with this tool, which is fitted with its own ruler to measure the width of the cut.

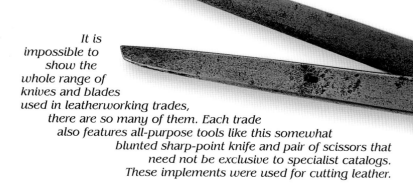

It is
impossible to
show the
whole range of
knives and blades
used in leatherworking trades,
there are so many of them. Each trade
also features all-purpose tools like this somewhat
blunted sharp-point knife and pair of scissors that
need not be exclusive to specialist catalogs.
These implements were used for cutting leather.

These steel
models belong to the
family of hole punchers
and are used for punching
strap ends. One has a smooth
sharp end, while the other is fluted.
These implements make it possible to
produce a series of identical products.

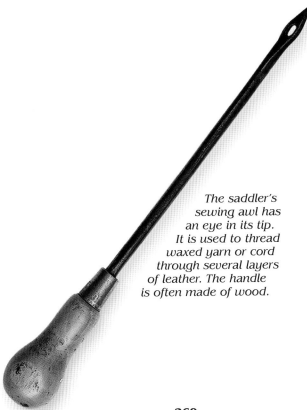

The saddler's sewing awl has an eye in its tip. It is used to thread waxed yarn or cord through several layers of leather. The handle is often made of wood.

This bronze wheel is different from the one on page 263, which is used to mark the position of stitching. This one is used for decorating the edges of leather belts and harnesses and is applied hot on damp leather.

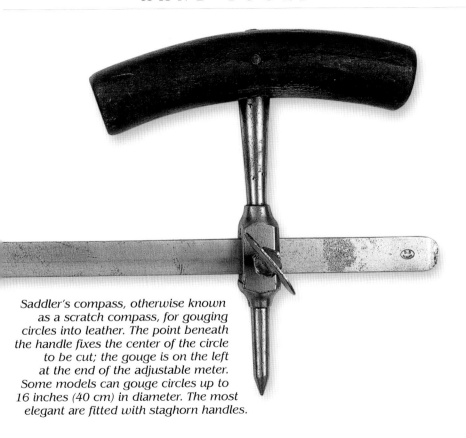

*Saddler's compass, otherwise known
as a scratch compass, for gouging
circles into leather. The point beneath
the handle fixes the center of the circle
to be cut; the gouge is on the left
at the end of the adjustable meter.
Some models can gouge circles up to
16 inches (40 cm) in diameter. The most
elegant are fitted with staghorn handles.*

This may look like an
implement for harvesting
cabbages, but most likely
it was used in the process
of currying leather, the stage
when tanned hides are oiled
and buffed for use. It probably served
to pull hides from the tanning vats.

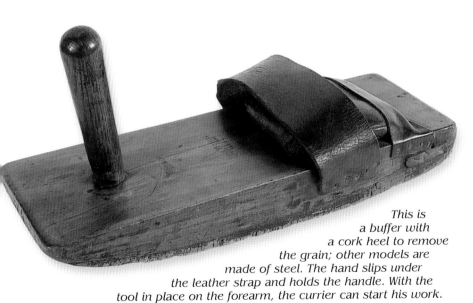

This is
a buffer with
a cork heel to remove
the grain; other models are
made of steel. The hand slips under
the leather strap and holds the handle. With the
tool in place on the forearm, the currier can start his work.

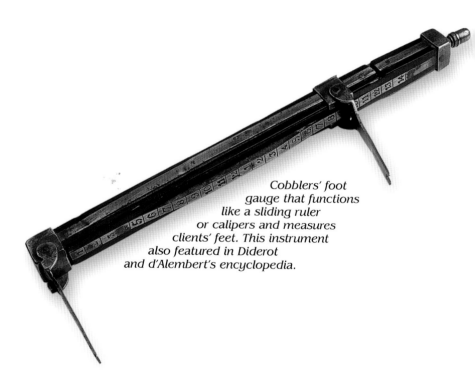

Cobblers' foot
gauge that functions
like a sliding ruler
or calipers and measures
clients' feet. This instrument
also featured in Diderot
and d'Alembert's encyclopedia.

For sewing hard to reach
seams, saddlers invented
this small wooden machine.
It functions with alternating
movements of the two handles
at the top. The needle is at the bottom.
In one move, the needle is inserted;
in the next it is withdrawn. This model is
made of beech wood with a steel needle.
This one dates from around 1920.

A basic saddlers' mallet, handy for a host of tasks, in particular shaping leather. Note the leather thong used to hang it on a wall alongside other tools in the leatherworker's arsenal.

Surely the tool most widely used by saddlers, cobblers, and all leatherworkers. After applying the pricking wheel, awls serve to bore holes through which waxed yarn is then threaded. The curved awl in the middle is marked Fernand Mayer, Paris. Mayer was at one time Blanchard's great competitor.

*Saddlers'
hole punches were
generally made of a single
block of iron. Some are made
of hardwood with a steel blade.
They were used for making harnesses
as well as for decoration.*

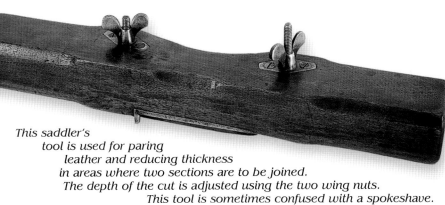

This saddler's tool is used for paring leather and reducing thickness in areas where two sections are to be joined. The depth of the cut is adjusted using the two wing nuts. This tool is sometimes confused with a spokeshave.

V

CONSTRUCTION
hand tools

I f ever there had to be a symbol of the
construction trade, the plumb line would be
a good candidate, with the carpenter's square
and compasses or mason's trowel as close runners-
up. The construction trade also draws on a host
of other trades to complete its tasks, which means
that its arsenal of tools is huge. Clay must be dug
from the ground before being turned into tiles
and bricks; wood must be cut for the carpenter
and glass cut for windows. Stone-cutters have
their own emblems, the mallet and chisel,
to symbolize their particular craft.

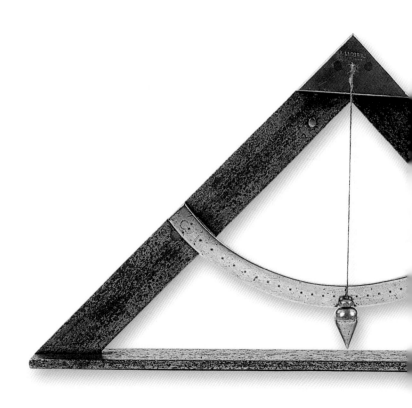

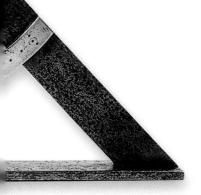

*Banking level made of steel from the end
of the nineteenth century, with a brass arc
and plumb line. "A. Lecorre" is etched
in the ninety-degree angle.*

*Rudimentary steel plumb level. To measure greater lengths
a ruler could be placed at its base. Facing page, a plumb level
for architects or land surveyors, working on the same principle.*

By looking through each hole in the top corners of the frame,
the eye can focus on a precise point, enabling measurement
of the incline between the viewing position and the point,
using the plumb line. This frame is made of cast iron
and dates from the start of the twentieth century.

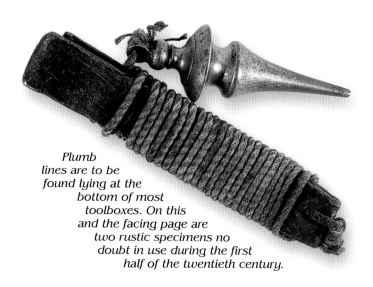

*Plumb
lines are to be
found lying at the
bottom of most
toolboxes. On this
and the facing page are
two rustic specimens no
doubt in use during the first
half of the twentieth century.*

The difference between these two plumb lines is that the axis of the line on the left does not actually pass through the center of the weight due to its hoop fixture.

In the 1899 Les Fils de Peugeot Frères catalog, there are no fewer than twenty-four pages devoted to trowels of all kinds. The catalog states that, "The trowel is an article with a variety of shapes depending on local custom. When ordering a trowel, you must specify the type, length of blade, width of tip and heel, and thickness, as well as the height of its stem."

The steel trowel on the facing page is a London trowel. The model on this page is a gauging trowel, used by plasterers. It is made of brass to avoid corrosion.

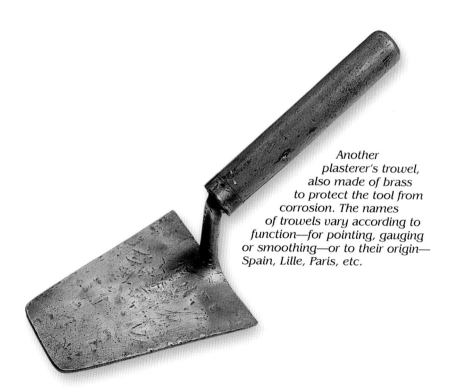

Another plasterer's trowel, also made of brass to protect the tool from corrosion. The names of trowels vary according to function—for pointing, gauging or smoothing—or to their origin— Spain, Lille, Paris, etc.

This jointing iron was devised for smoothing cement between bricks. The metal-clad foot is passed over the wet cement in the gaps.

Plasterers, as well as stonecutters working soft stone,
use this kind of tool. The rabbet plane is used
in the same way as its counterpart in the carpenter's
workshop. The craftsman who used this model
marked it with his initials, A. L.

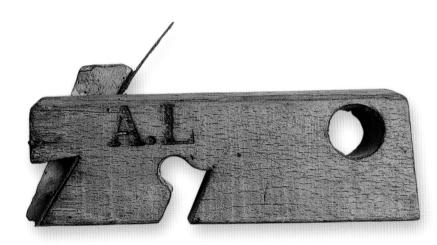

*This rabbet plane is for use on plaster and soft stone.
Note the double blades, with one on the butt, to plane
down the plaster right into the corners.*

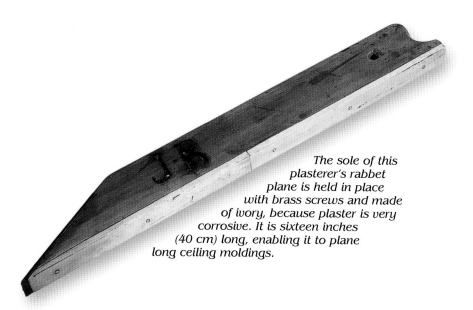

The sole of this plasterer's rabbet plane is held in place with brass screws and made of ivory, because plaster is very corrosive. It is sixteen inches (40 cm) long, enabling it to plane long ceiling moldings.

This is a plastering trowel. While its handle is made of sturdy boxwood, its blade and stem are made of brass because of the corrosiveness of the materials being worked.

This particular form of hammer is specific to the slate-quarrying and roofing trades. Note the knife-like cutting edge on the shaft. The pointed peen serves to trace striking lines as well as to pierce slate.

This nail-puller is used by roofers to slip beneath roof slates and remove the nails holding them in place.

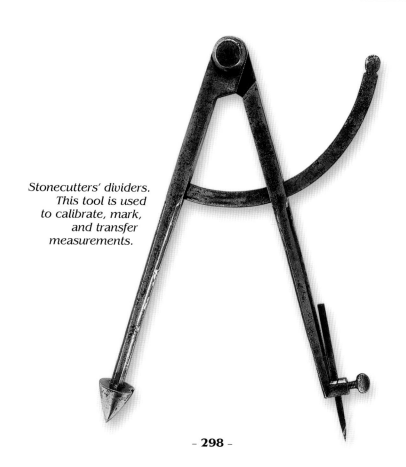

*Stonecutters' dividers.
This tool is used
to calibrate, mark,
and transfer
measurements.*

A number of trades use this type of hammer, in particular masons; their version would have rounded peens, however. This particular model probably belonged to a stone cutter.

The bush-hammer has diamond-shaped teeth, used for smoothing and finishing a hewn stone.

The sandstone "comb" used by the stone cutter often had eleven removable teeth, held in place by a wedge. This meant that worn or broken teeth could be replaced or adjusted to fit a given profile. Note the handle made from a series of leather hoops.

AU VILLAGE

MARÉCHAL FERRANT.

1. Vous êtes maréchal de France tout d'même

V

AMAZING
hand tools

There are so many unusual tools that they deserve a whole chapter to themselves. To the novice, they might appear strange, even eccentric, and their function is not always easy to determine. Think of this chapter as a kind of quiz, a chance to broaden the scope of your knowledge, or confirm what you already know about a set of intriguing objects that may not be what they seem. From the hat-stretching block to the setting-clamp, via the date stamp or flower-maker's tongs, there is a wonderful world to be discovered in flea markets and antique shops everywhere.

This is a weaver's comb. The two holes on each side hold the comb out of the way as the shuttle passes.

This is an old-fashioned meat tenderizer. The steak was first worked between the jaws of this implement before it was slipped under the grill.

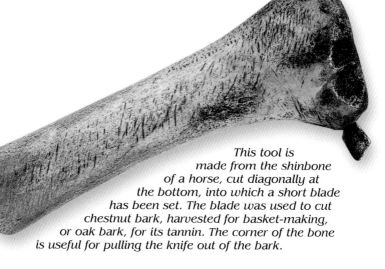

This tool is
made from the shinbone
of a horse, cut diagonally at
the bottom, into which a short blade
has been set. The blade was used to cut
chestnut bark, harvested for basket-making,
or oak bark, for its tannin. The corner of the bone
is useful for pulling the knife out of the bark.

The wheelwright's wheel or gauge is a measuring instrument used for measuring the length of curves. The zero point is marked by the cloverleaf.

Woodcutters' marking
hammer, for printing
a number directly onto
the sapwood of trunks
once the bark has been
removed with the
woodcutters' axe.

This tool has the same function as that on the facing page but does not allow for a combination of numbers in the same strike. Signed "Wilh. Göhler's W. Freiberg."

This is a household implement,
used to make briquettes of
coal from residual coal dust.
A handy tool for recycling.

Shoelaces used to be sold by the yard. This implement stamps and seals their ends to allow them to slip easily through lace holes. It was made by Daudé, in Paris, and dates from the start of the twentieth century.

*This is a
specialist saw for
working horn, a material
extensively used by comb manufacturers
and by knife-makers for handles. Zinc workers
also have their own curved or triangular
version of the implement.*

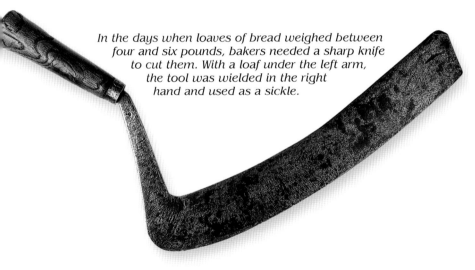

In the days when loaves of bread weighed between four and six pounds, bakers needed a sharp knife to cut them. With a loaf under the left arm, the tool was wielded in the right hand and used as a sickle.

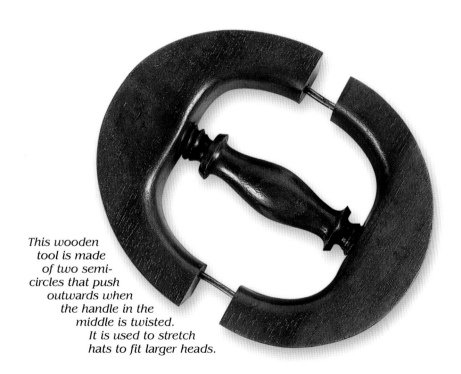

This wooden tool is made of two semi-circles that push outwards when the handle in the middle is twisted. It is used to stretch hats to fit larger heads.

This hat-stretching block is made of lime wood and was used for working damp felt. The two halves come apart down the middle when the handle is turned.

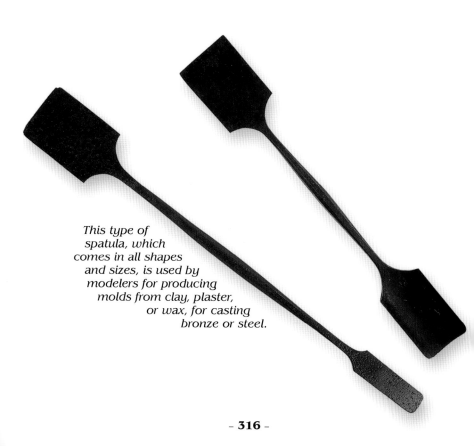

This type of spatula, which comes in all shapes and sizes, is used by modelers for producing molds from clay, plaster, or wax, for casting bronze or steel.

*This mallet was made
of cow horn and a chestnut
twig and could well be
homemade. It was used
for cracking nuts.*

This was a miller's
tool used for
rejuvenating worn
millstones, by chipping away
at the grooves and furrows
left by the grinding of wheat,
barley, rye, or buckwheat.

*This tool, half adze, half gouge,
was used to fashion ox yokes
from beech, ash, alder,
or whatever hardwood
grew locally.*

This
tool from the
mid-twentieth century,
marked Garanto-Skai-DRP,
is used to set saw teeth,
giving each an alternating
lateral angle.

Stonecutter's knife for repairing joints. The body and blade are made of steel and the blade is adjustable according to the depth required.

Boring and gouging
instruments are legion.
Each has its own specific
function. This one is used
for manufacturing pianos
and stringed instruments.
The handle of this model from
the start of the twentieth century
is made of hardwood.

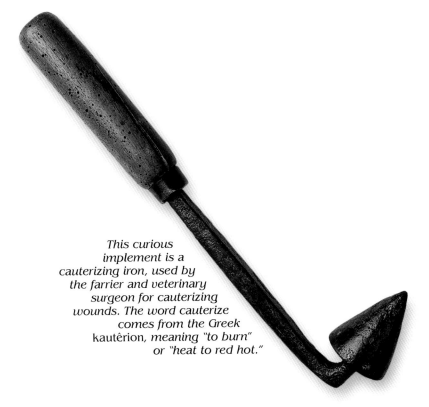

This curious
implement is a
cauterizing iron, used by
the farrier and veterinary
surgeon for cauterizing
wounds. The word cauterize
comes from the Greek
kautêrion, meaning "to burn"
or "heat to red hot."

Horn was a
common material
for the comb
manufacturer, and this
clamp was used to bend
warm strips of horn
to make ladies' hairgrips.

This unusual pick is used for caulking boats. The large curved blade pushes the caulk between the planks to seal the hull. Note that this model has a dual purpose as the handle has a pry bar fitting.

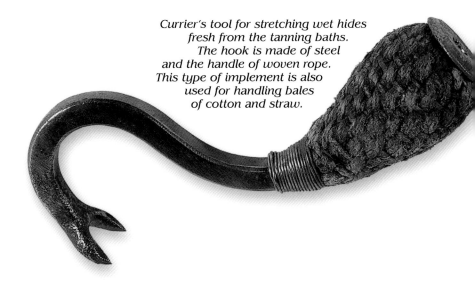

*Currier's tool for stretching wet hides
fresh from the tanning baths.
The hook is made of steel
and the handle of woven rope.
This type of implement is also
used for handling bales
of cotton and straw.*

Glassmakers would stamp bottles using bronze tools like these. They would affix a red hot lozenge of glass to the finished bottle and stamp it with their seal.

This pruning hook is unusual in that it has three sharp blades in a single tool, offering different angles for pushing and pulling branches. The end of the spatula and the two crescents have been sharpened for snagging smaller branches and pulling them to the ground.

This utensil is a kind of bread knife. The large slab of bread is held beneath the arm and the blade cuts off shavings of bread to thicken soup.

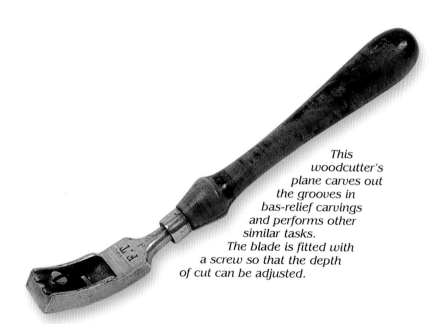

This woodcutter's plane carves out the grooves in bas-relief carvings and performs other similar tasks. The blade is fitted with a screw so that the depth of cut can be adjusted.

This pounder was used for setting paving stones into place. There were two sizes of pounder; the larger one was used standing while its smaller sibling was used kneeling. The base of the pounder is covered in large round-headed nails.

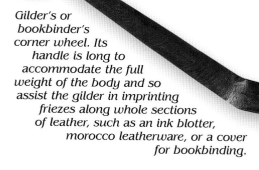

Gilder's or bookbinder's corner wheel. Its handle is long to accommodate the full weight of the body and so assist the gilder in imprinting friezes along whole sections of leather, such as an ink blotter, morocco leatherware, or a cover for bookbinding.

This instrument is a gilder's stamp for printing initials or titles on leather. The bronze letters forming a word or name are held in place by the screw in the shaft at the bottom. The stamp is used cold on damp leather. The letters are then gilded.

Like the tool on the preceding page for imprinting
words, these gilders' irons were used for decorating
book covers and engraving initials, etc.

This is a
bookbinder's
saw used for
making notches
on the back of
assembled sheets of
manuscript to help them
stick to their binding.

Shears such as these
feature in Diderot
and d'Alembert's eighteenth-
century encyclopedia,
which is not surprising
as they do indeed
date from the period.
They are tailors' scissors
for cutting cloth.

*A pair of compasses
with a fitted draw-chisel
blade from the eighteenth
century used by cabinetmakers
for working decorations
into wood. On one side
is a point and on the other
a draw-chisel blade.*

The wooden-headed mallet
serves to show the scale
of this jewelers' anvil,
which was used for
working and shaping
precious metals.

These pincers are for flowers, not the natural blooming kind, but the artificial variety, produced at the start of the twentieth century. Note the bird's head at the tip of the handle.

*The principle of the steelyard is simple.
The weight attached to the chain slides
along the scaled arm, while wares
to be weighed are slung over the hook.
The upper ring is used to hang the balance.
The ring below is for fitting
a tare if necessary.*

*A balance
working on the
same principle as the
steelyard on the facing page. This model is more
elaborate as it has a spring-loaded needle to
indicate weight on a graduated dial made of brass.*

This spring balance dates from the start of the twentieth century and is graduated from one to one hundred kilos (2.2 to 220 pounds).

*This unusual implement was used by glove-makers
for scraping their fine leathers. The handle
is wooden while the scraper
is made of glass.*

This
small plane
has a specific use that is not
immediately evident. It was used
by hat-makers to cut or trim the edge
of felt hats. On the frame is etched
the brand name: Oradour, Paris.

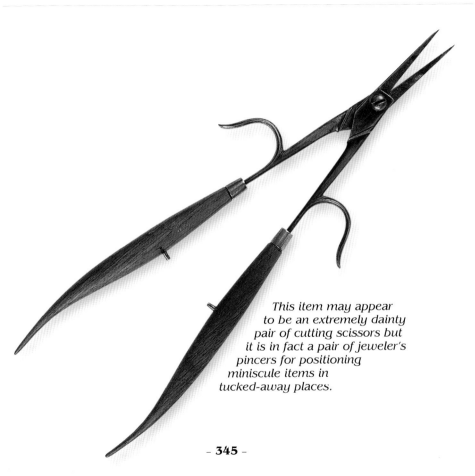

*This item may appear
to be an extremely dainty
pair of cutting scissors but
it is in fact a pair of jeweler's
pincers for positioning
miniscule items in
tucked-away places.*

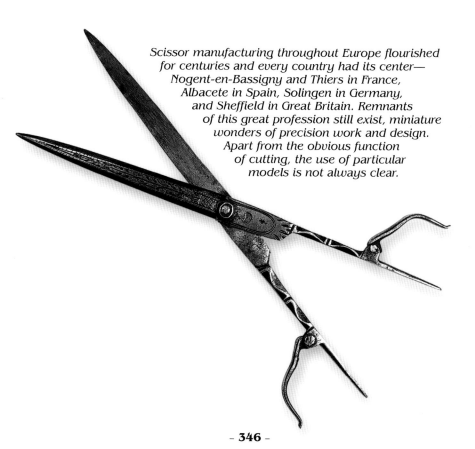

Scissor manufacturing throughout Europe flourished
for centuries and every country had its center—
Nogent-en-Bassigny and Thiers in France,
Albacete in Spain, Solingen in Germany,
and Sheffield in Great Britain. Remnants
of this great profession still exist, miniature
wonders of precision work and design.
Apart from the obvious function
of cutting, the use of particular
models is not always clear.

*Bucket-makers,
manufacturers
of wooden pails, used
scrapers and small straight
and curved planes of this kind.
Long handles were necessary to
reach the bottom of tall buckets.*

Jewelers use this kind of cone gauge for measuring the diameter of rings.

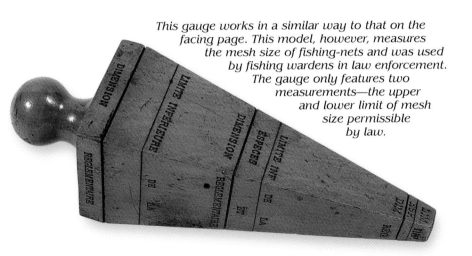

This gauge works in a similar way to that on the facing page. This model, however, measures the mesh size of fishing-nets and was used by fishing wardens in law enforcement. The gauge only features two measurements—the upper and lower limit of mesh size permissible by law.

The cooper
would use this
gouge, with its steel
blade and long handle,
for smoothing the bottom
of the staves in a barrel.
The length of its handle must
have made it a difficult
instrument to use.

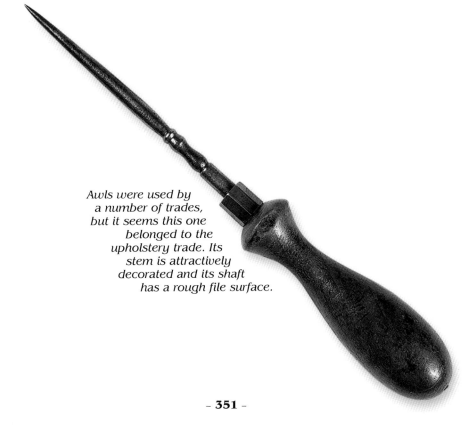

*Awls were used by
a number of trades,
but it seems this one
belonged to the
upholstery trade. Its
stem is attractively
decorated and its shaft
has a rough file surface.*

This woodcutter's draw-chisel is used to mark trees by digging the blade (on the left) into the bark or sapwood. The curved metal hook on the right folds over the handle to protect the hand when in use.

*This
attractive pair of
calipers in the shape
of a figure eight is similar
to the "dancing-master,"
page 203, and is a
clock-maker's tool.*

In the nineteenth century, sugar was not sold in neat cubes in tight-fitting boxes; it was sold in three-pound (1.5 kilo) blocks. A small axe was used to score it before pincers finished off the job.

A pair of pincers for cutting sugar, with blades of the same shape as the sugar axe on the facing page. This model is made of forged steel and dates from the nineteenth century, like the axe on the facing page, which has a plane wood handle.

This peculiar mechanism is a winegrower's clasp. The prongs pierce the trunk of the vine and stop the sap rising.

This is a cooper's
mallet with its
characteristic long
handle made of flexible
wood such as walnut,
ash, bamboo, or reed.
With one brisk strike on
the cask with the mallet,
it was possible to
remove the bung.

The basket-maker would use these cleavers
for splitting wicker. Three notches would be cut into
the tip of the branch, then the cleaver would complete
the work down its length, producing three separate
lengths of wicker for the construction of baskets
and other wares. The cleavers were
generally made of boxwood.

These curious iron implements
were used to shape the artificial
flowers that decorated women's
hats and filled their vases
in the early 1900s.

These are molds rather like waffle-irons, with male and female sections, for making artificial flowers. Plant-fiber based materials were used...

...and the two sections fitted together to press them into highly realistic ornaments. They were generally made of brass or bronze.

*Thousands
of these leaves were
produced, to the
delight of women
and men alike,
in the first quarter
of the twentieth century.*

Before petals or leaves were molded,
they needed cutting out. Punches like
these were struck with a mallet
to produce the initial outlines.

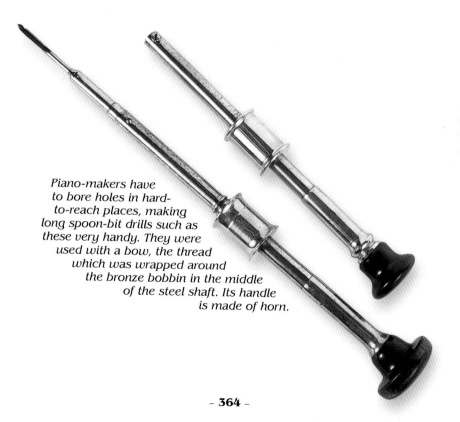

Piano-makers have
to bore holes in hard-
to-reach places, making
long spoon-bit drills such as
these very handy. They were
used with a bow, the thread
which was wrapped around
the bronze bobbin in the middle
of the steel shaft. Its handle
is made of horn.

Hammers for inlaying and veneering have much the same form and both have a wide peen. The only difference is their material— veneering hammers are made of wood while their inlaying counterpart uses steel.

Among our amazing tools this magnificently worked nineteenth-century clock-maker's oil holder. Clock-makers use a special, particularly refined oil.

This is not a backscratcher but a mason's jointer, used for introducing wet plaster, cement, lime or other near-liquid material between stones, bricks or rubblework.

The metal shreds, or swarf, that remain on chisels
or gouges after sharpening needs to be removed if the tool
is to cut perfectly. This machine removes those shreds
and is adapted for bevels of all dimensions.

Carding wool, to give it body before using it to stuff mattresses or spin, is a long, tedious task performed with these carding combs. Carding has the same root as the French "chardon" or thistle. The plant, with its natural hooks, was once used for the same purpose.

Addresses
and
References

Index

The index lists the main proper names and tool names that appear in the text.

INDEX

INDEX

Acknowledgments and Addresses

First, I would like to thank the Amis de l'outil in Bièvres outside Paris. They are a non-profit association who have opened a marvelous museum dedicated to antique tools and the memory of manual labor. Many of the photos illustrating this book were taken there. I am indebted to their members' kindness. I wish to express my gratitude to the Chairman of the association, Jean-François Delangle, and to their curator, Daniel Lesoimier, who gave up so much of his time to help us.

Musée de l'Outil ancien, place de l'Église - 91570 Bièvres, France
Tel. and fax: 00 33 (0)1 69 85 31 26
Internet site: http://lado.asso.free.fr
Open Saturday and Sunday, the second and fourth weeks of each month, from 2 pm to 6 pm and by appointment, twenty people minimum.
Every year, to celebrate May 1st, Labor Day, the association stages a huge antique tool fair in the streets of the village.

Many thanks too to the L' Herminette store where we dug up a number of interesting tools.
Le Louvre des antiquaires, 2, place du Palais Royal - 75001 Paris, France.
Tel.: 00 33 (0)1 42 61 57 81

Thanks to Christian Monnier and Jean-Louis Laine, coordinators for "Aventure Peugeot," a body that governs collections of the Peugeot group's heritage.
Musée Peugeot, Carrefour de l'Europe - 25600 Sochaux, France
Tel.: 00 33 (0)3 81 94 48 21

My thoughts go out too to all the local hand tool and craft museums scattered around France, which so often exist only because of the enthusiasm of an individual or couple. One such museum is to be found in the village of Wy-dit-Joli in Val-d'Oise, run by Claude Pigeard and his wife Françoise, both of whom have taught me so much.

The Sloane-Stanley Museum, has a particularly interesting collection of early American tools.
Sloane-Stanley Museum, Route 7, P.O. Box 917, Kent, Connecticut 06757, USA
Tel.: (860) 927 3849

The website www.antiquetools.com is a good resource for anyone interested in tools.

Bibliography

– *Daniel Boucard*. Les Outils de métiers. *Éditions Jean-Cyrille Godefroy, 2002.*

– *Daniel Boucard*. Les Outils taillants. *Éditions Jean-Cyrille Godefroy, 2000.*

– *Daniel Boucard*. Les Haches. *Éditions Jean-Cyrille Godefroy, 1998.*

– *André Mercuzot*. Guide des outils. *Éditions Jean-Cyrille Godefroy, 1997.*

– *Roger Verdier*. Glossaire du collectionneur d'outils.
Éditions du cabinet d'expertises, 1996.

– *Jean-Claude Frouard and Roger Verdier*. L'Outil du XVIIe au XXe siècle,
de la fonction à la collection, catalogue d'exposition. *1985.*

– *Paul Feller and Fernand Tourret*. L' Outil, dialogue de l'homme avec la matière.
Éditions Albert de Visscher, 1969.

– *The "Fils de Peugeot Frères" general catalogs of 1899 and 1926,
as well as various other hand tool catalogs
from the nineteenth and twentieth centuries.*

In the same collection

Collectible Eyeglasses
by Frédérique Crestin-Billet
ISBN: 2-0803-0437-2

Collectible Wristwatches
by René Pannier
ISBN: 2-0801-0621-X

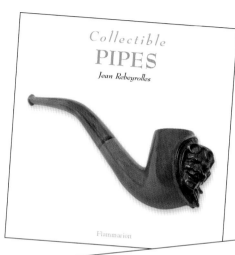

Collectible Pipes
by Jean Rebeyrolles
ISBN: 2-0801-0884-0

Collectible Lighters
by Juan Manuel Clark
ISBN: 2-0801-1133-7

Collectible Pocket Knives
by Dominique Pascal
ISBN: 2-0801-0550-7

Collectible
CORKSCREWS
Frédérique Crestin-Billet

Flammarion

Collectible
MINIATURE
PERFUME BOTTLES

Anne Breton

Flammarion

Collectible
FOUNTAIN
PENS
Juan Manuel Clark

Flammarion

Collectible Corkscrews
by Frédérique Crestin–Billet
ISBN: 2-0801-0551-5

*Collectible Miniature
Perfume Bottles*
by Anne Breton
ISBN: 2-0801-0632-5

Collectible Fountain Pens
by Juan Manuel Clark
ISBN: 2-0801-0719-4

Collectible Miniature Cars
by Dominique Pascal
ISBN: 2-0801-0718-6

Collectible Model Trains
by David-Paul Gurney
ISBN: 2-081-1142-6

Collectible Snowdomes
by Lélie Carnot
ISBN: 2-0801-0889-1

Collectible Playing Cards
by Frédérique Crestin-Billet
ISBN: 2-0801-1134-5

Collectible Toy Soldiers
by Dominique Pascal
ISBN: 2-0801-1141-8

Collectible
PLAYING CARDS

Frédérique Crestin-Billet

Flammarion

Collectible
TOY
SOLDIERS

Dominique Pascal

Flammarion

Photo credits